Assessment, Accreditation and Ranking Methods for Higher Education Institutes in India: Current Findings and Future Challenges

Edited by

Sankara Narayana Rao Gedala

&

P.L. Saranya

Department of Physics
Goverment College for Women Autonomous Srikakulam
Dr. B.R. Ambedkar University
Srikakulam, A.P.
India

Assessment, Accreditation and Ranking Methods for Higher Education Institutes in India: Current Findings and Future Challenges

Editors: Sankara Narayana Rao Gedala and P.L. Saranya

ISBN (Online): 978-1-68108-817-4

ISBN (Print): 978-1-68108-818-1

ISBN (Paperback): 978-1-68108-819-8

© 2021, Bentham Books imprint.

Published by Bentham Science Publishers – Sharjah, UAE. All Rights Reserved.

BENTHAM SCIENCE PUBLISHERS LTD.
End User License Agreement (for non-institutional, personal use)

This is an agreement between you and Bentham Science Publishers Ltd. Please read this License Agreement carefully before using the ebook/echapter/ejournal (**"Work"**). Your use of the Work constitutes your agreement to the terms and conditions set forth in this License Agreement. If you do not agree to these terms and conditions then you should not use the Work.

Bentham Science Publishers agrees to grant you a non-exclusive, non-transferable limited license to use the Work subject to and in accordance with the following terms and conditions. This License Agreement is for non-library, personal use only. For a library / institutional / multi user license in respect of the Work, please contact: permission@benthamscience.net.

Usage Rules:

1. All rights reserved: The Work is 1. the subject of copyright and Bentham Science Publishers either owns the Work (and the copyright in it) or is licensed to distribute the Work. You shall not copy, reproduce, modify, remove, delete, augment, add to, publish, transmit, sell, resell, create derivative works from, or in any way exploit the Work or make the Work available for others to do any of the same, in any form or by any means, in whole or in part, in each case without the prior written permission of Bentham Science Publishers, unless stated otherwise in this License Agreement.
2. You may download a copy of the Work on one occasion to one personal computer (including tablet, laptop, desktop, or other such devices). You may make one back-up copy of the Work to avoid losing it.
3. The unauthorised use or distribution of copyrighted or other proprietary content is illegal and could subject you to liability for substantial money damages. You will be liable for any damage resulting from your misuse of the Work or any violation of this License Agreement, including any infringement by you of copyrights or proprietary rights.

Disclaimer:

Bentham Science Publishers does not guarantee that the information in the Work is error-free, or warrant that it will meet your requirements or that access to the Work will be uninterrupted or error-free. The Work is provided "as is" without warranty of any kind, either express or implied or statutory, including, without limitation, implied warranties of merchantability and fitness for a particular purpose. The entire risk as to the results and performance of the Work is assumed by you. No responsibility is assumed by Bentham Science Publishers, its staff, editors and/or authors for any injury and/or damage to persons or property as a matter of products liability, negligence or otherwise, or from any use or operation of any methods, products instruction, advertisements or ideas contained in the Work.

Limitation of Liability:

In no event will Bentham Science Publishers, its staff, editors and/or authors, be liable for any damages, including, without limitation, special, incidental and/or consequential damages and/or damages for lost data and/or profits arising out of (whether directly or indirectly) the use or inability to use the Work. The entire liability of Bentham Science Publishers shall be limited to the amount actually paid by you for the Work.

General:

1. Any dispute or claim arising out of or in connection with this License Agreement or the Work (including non-contractual disputes or claims) will be governed by and construed in accordance with the laws of the U.A.E. as applied in the Emirate of Dubai. Each party agrees that the courts of the Emirate of Dubai shall have exclusive jurisdiction to settle any dispute or claim arising out of or in connection with this License Agreement or the Work (including non-contractual disputes or claims).
2. Your rights under this License Agreement will automatically terminate without notice and without the

need for a court order if at any point you breach any terms of this License Agreement. In no event will any delay or failure by Bentham Science Publishers in enforcing your compliance with this License Agreement constitute a waiver of any of its rights.

3. You acknowledge that you have read this License Agreement, and agree to be bound by its terms and conditions. To the extent that any other terms and conditions presented on any website of Bentham Science Publishers conflict with, or are inconsistent with, the terms and conditions set out in this License Agreement, you acknowledge that the terms and conditions set out in this License Agreement shall prevail.

Bentham Science Publishers Ltd.
Executive Suite Y - 2
PO Box 7917, Saif Zone
Sharjah, U.A.E.
Email: subscriptions@benthamscience.net

CONTENTS

FOREWORD	i
PREFACE	ii
LIST OF CONTRIBUTORS	iii
CHAPTER 1 CHALLENGES OF HIGHER EDUCATION INSTITUTIONS IN ASSESSMENT ACCREDITATION AND RANKING FRAMEWORK METHODOLOGIES	1
K. Sreeramulu	
INTRODUCTION	1
CHALLENGES OF THE PRESENT HIGHER EDUCATIONAL SYSTEM IN INDIA-SUGGESTIONS	3
Industry and Academia Connection	4
Incentives to Teachers and Researchers	4
Action Plan for Quality Improvement	4
Student-Centered Education and Dynamic Methods	4
Need Based Job-Oriented Courses	5
Holistic Development	5
Accreditation and Rankings	6
CONCLUSION	6
CONSENT FOR PUBLICATION	7
CONFLICT OF INTEREST	7
ACKNOWLEDGEMENTS	7
REFERENCES	7
CHAPTER 2 CAN A STUDENT FEEDBACK PROVIDE CORRECT OPINION ON TEACHING-LEARNING PROCESS IN HIGHER EDUCATION INSTITUTES?	8
G. Sankaranarayana Rao	
INTRODUCTION	8
METHODOLOGY	11
RESULTS AND DISCUSSIONS	18
CONCLUDING REMARKS	21
CONSENT FOR PUBLICATION	21
CONFLICT OF INTEREST	21
ACKNOWLEDGEMENTS	22
REFERENCES	22
CHAPTER 3 A & A - QUANTITATIVE METRICS - A BIRD'S EYE VIEW	25
K. Mythili	
INTRODUCTION	25
STUDY METHOD	27
NAAC Methodology and Challenges of HEI	27
Criterion I: Curricular Aspects	27
Criterion II- Teaching, Learning, and Evaluation	28
Criterion III- Research, Innovations and Extension	29
Criterion IV-Infrastructure and Learning Resources	30
Criterion V-Student Support and Progression	30
Criterion VI-Governance, Leadership and Management	30
Criterion VI-Institutional Values and Social Responsibilities	31
Optional Metrics-Rules & Regulations	31
CONCLUSION	32
CONSENT FOR PUBLICATION	33

CONFLICT OF INTEREST	33
ACKNOWLEDGEMENTS	33
REFERENCES	33

CHAPTER 4 PROMINENCE OF STUDENT SUPPORT AND PROGRESSION IN THE NAAC ASSESSMENT FOR QUALITY AUGMENTATION IN HIGHER EDUCATION INSTITUTIONS OF ANDHRA PRADESH INDIA 34
Smt. T. Kasiratnam and Smt. R.S. Goldina

INTRODUCTION	34
NAAC METHODOLOGY: STUDENT SUPPORT AND PROGRESSION	36
Curriculum Feedback	36
Maintenance of Ward Register	36
Group Learning	37
ANALYSIS: NAAC ASSESSMENT OF COLLEGES	37
Student Progression	39
Student Participation	40
CONCLUSION	40
CONSENT FOR PUBLICATION	41
CONFLICT OF INTEREST	41
ACKNOWLEDGEMENTS	41
REFERENCES	41

CHAPTER 5 HIGHER RECOMPENSE TO THE HIGHLY QUALIFIED – A WAY TO ECONOMIC DEVELOPMENT 42
P.L. Saranya, N.V.S. Bhagavan and B. Preethi

INTRODUCTION	42
GLOBAL TRENDS FOR INVESTMENTS IN INTELLECTUAL CAPITAL	44
Higher Education in India	46
Proposed Structural Changes in the Education System in India	47
Suggested Learning Methodologies	48
CONCLUSION	49
CONSENT FOR PUBLICATION	49
CONFLICT OF INTEREST	49
ACKNOWLEDGEMENTS	49
REFERENCES	49

CHAPTER 6 ROLE OF DIGITIZATION IN HIGHER EDUCATIONAL INSTITUTIONS FOR BETTER RANKING & EMPLOYABILITY 51
B.V.A.N.S.S. Prabhakar Rao

INTRODUCTION	52
MODERN METHODS – DELIVERY OF CONTENT	52
LITERATURE REVIEW	53
PROPOSED SYSTEM	54
CONCLUSION	58
CONSENT FOR PUBLICATION	58
CONFLICT OF INTEREST	58
ACKNOWLEDGEMENTS	58
REFERENCES	58

CHAPTER 7 EDUCATION "RE" CREATION 61
M.R. Joginaidu and M.J.A. Swaroop

INTRODUCTION	61
CHALLENGES AND SOLUTIONS	63

Learning Stages and Possible Approaches	63
Early Childhood Care and Education {1 to 6 Years}	64
Identify Natural Gifts and Passion {7 to 17 Years}	64
Passion Achieving {17 to 25 Years}	65
Lifelong Adventure	65
CONCLUSION	65
CONSENT FOR PUBLICATION	66
CONFLICT OF INTEREST	66
ACKNOWLEDGEMENTS	66
REFERENCES	66
CHAPTER 8 IMPORTANCE OF PROFESSIONAL LIFE SKILLS	67
K. Suryachandra Rao	
INTRODUCTION	67
BENEFITS FOR THE INDIVIDUALS	68
Skill Development in Today's World	69
COMMUNICATION SKILLS	69
Listening	70
Nonverbal Communication	70
Clarity and Precision	70
Affable Personality	70
Confidence	71
Empathy	71
Open –mindedness	71
Respect	71
Feedback	71
Picking the Right Medium	72
LIFE SKILLS	72
Problem Solving	72
Emotional Intelligence	72
Emotional Competence	73
Self-awareness	73
Emotional Regulation	73
Resilence	74
Trustworthiness and Conscientiousness	74
Fortitude	74
Flexibility	74
Innovation	75
Drive to Achieve	75
Sensitivity	75
Social Competence	75
Team Work	75
Adaptability	76
Assertive Skills	76
Stress Management	76
Positive Attitude	77
Creativity	77
I.T SKILLS	77
CONCLUSION	78
CONSENT FOR PUBLICATION	78
CONFLICT OF INTEREST	78

ACKNOWLEDGEMENTS	78
REFERENCES	78

CHAPTER 9 LEVERAGING ICT FOR EXCELLENCE IN HIGHER EDUCATION INSTITUTIONS USING STANDARDS AND CRITERIA OF ACCREDITATION AND RANKING 80
Pradeep Kumar, Balvinder Shukla and *Don Passey*

INTRODUCTION	80
ACCREDITATION AND RANKING	82
Before Applying	84
Submission of Initial Application	84
Submission of a Detailed Report	84
Data Validation and Verification (DVV) Process	84
Satisfaction Survey	84
Site Visit	84
Declaration of Result	85
Public Disclosure of Information	85
Submission of Annual Report and Annual Dues	85
Role of ICT in Higher Education	86
Leveraging ICT in Accreditation and Rankings of Higher Education Institutions	88
Methodology	91
Statistical Techniques used for Data Analysis	91
Findings and Discussions	92
CONCLUSION	94
CONSENT FOR PUBLICATION	95
CONFLICT OF INTEREST	95
ACKNOWLEDGEMENTS	95
REFERENCES	95

CHAPTER 10 IMPACT OF GLOBALIZATION ON HIGHER EDUCATION-A COMPARATIVE STUDY BETWEEN PUBLIC AND PRIVATE UNIVERSITIES 98
M.R. Jyothifrederick

INTRODUCTION	98
NEED AND SIGNIFICANCE OF THE STUDY	100
METHODOLOGY	101
DATA ANALYSIS	101
Services	102
Innovations	103
Quality Measures	106
External Exposure	107
Policy Measures	109
MAJOR FINDINGS	111
CONCLUSION	112
CONSENT FOR PUBLICATION	113
CONFLICT OF INTEREST	113
ACKNOWLEDGEMENTS	113
REFERENCES	113

CHAPTER 11 CHALLENGES AND PROSPECTS OF HIGHER EDUCATION IN INDIA 115
Smt. M. Santhi and *Smt. T. Adilakshmi*

INTRODUCTION	115
PRESENT SCENARIO OF HIGHER EDUCATION SYSTEM IN INDIA	118

PROBLEMS AND CHALLENGES OF HIGHER EDUCATION SYSTEM IN INDIA	121
PROSPECTS OF HIGHER EDUCATION	125
SUGGESTIONS TO IMPROVE THE QUALITY OF HIGHER EDUCATION	126
CONCLUSION	126
CONSENT FOR PUBLICATION	127
CONFLICT OF INTEREST	127
ACKNOWLEDGEMENTS	127
REFERENCES	127

CHAPTER 12 PERFORMANCE OF HIGHER EDUCATION IN INDIA 128
K. Chakrapati

INTRODUCTION	128
ISSUES WITH HIGHER EDUCATION IN INDIA	129
Teaching Quality	129
Privatization	129
Quota System	129
Political Factors	130
Moral Issues	130
Challenges in Higher Education	130
Shortage of Resources	130
Vacancies in Teaching	130
Accountability and Performance of Teachers	131
LACK OF EMPLOYABLE SKILLS	131
THE MOST COMMON CHALLENGES	131
SUGGESTIONS FOR IMPROVING THE QUALITY OF HIGHER EDUCATION	132
CONCLUSION	132
CONSENT FOR PUBLICATION	133
CONFLICT OF INTEREST	133
ACKNOWLEDGEMENTS	133
REFERENCES	133

CHAPTER 13 HIGHER EDUCATION IN INDIA - ISSUES AND CHALLENGES 134
Godavari Venkata Murali Mohan

INTRODUCTION	134
HIGHER EDUCATION IN INDIA SINCE INDEPENDENCE	135
CHALLENGES	136
OPPORTUNITIES AHEAD	137
CONCLUSION	138
CONSENT FOR PUBLICATION	139
CONFLICT OF INTEREST	139
ACKNOWLEDGEMENTS	139
REFERENCES	139

CHAPTER 14 CHARACTERISTICS OF TEACHING AND LEARNING - A STUDY ON CHALLENGES 140
A. Ramarao and *Karri Rama Rao*

INTRODUCTION	140
OBSERVATIONS	141
Characteristics of Teaching and Learning	141
RESULTS AND DISCUSSION	142
CONCLUSION	143
CONSENT FOR PUBLICATION	143

CONFLICT OF INTEREST	143
ACKNOWLEDGEMENTS	143
REFERENCES	144
CHAPTER 15 NEW TEACHING-LEARNING METHODOLOGIES GLOBALIZATION	**145**
Srinivasa Babu Ampalam1,* and Pulakhandam Srinivasa Rao1	145
INTRODUCTION	146
CONCLUSION	151
CONSENT FOR PUBLICATION	151
CONFLICT OF INTEREST	152
ACKNOWLEDGEMENTS	152
REFERENCES	152
SUBJECT INDEX	**153**

FOREWORD

Higher Education has undergone rapid changes in the recent decade. There is a lot of transformation in the methods of teaching, learning, research and out reach activities. The present teaching learning experiences are augmented by ICT enabled methods and online courses MOOCS. The quality consciousness is increasing among the stakeholders. The growth of the institutes largely depends on the level of utilization of ICT enabled procedures, adopting the current trends in global education and redrawing their academic strategic plans suiting their local needs. The curriculum of the colleges should give a space to the students for acquiring employable skills and progression to higher education and research. The colleges/universities are expected to facilitate a vibrant, evolving ecosystem of innovative ideas. The institutes must reach to this level and provide education what the today's world demands and improve academic performance through the intelligent use of information technology to enhance learning. The students must catch up the local employment opportunities with these strategies. This book volume is a right step with this direction to share the experiences of the teachers, students and administrators in the Indian context.

I am happy to write this foreword, not only because some of the authors are experienced, friends and colleagues for more than thirty years, but also because I believe the book chapters discussed all aspects of the education institutes. I also believe that teachers at every stage of their career can enrich and strengthen their teaching by learning the discussion, presented in this book. Contributors of this book offer good examples to explore important questions and new ideas. These ideas can serve as a starting point for stake holders that will strengthen the learning experience for students and the institutions of higher education. I hope it will inspire readers.

In short, the book offers a learning experience on the institute accreditation methods, ranking procedures and innovative pedagogy. I hope that this book will become a primer for teachers, students, teacher educators and administrators to achieve a better grade.

Prof. S. Hara Sreeramulu
Ex Director Indian Institute of Information Technology, Srikakulam, A.P.
Principal Scientist MITS School of Bio-Technology, Utkal University, Bhubaneswar,
Coordinator of Bio-Technology, Dr. V.S. Krishna Govt. Degree College (Autonomous),
Visakhapatnam
India

PREFACE

Higher education systems are undergoing a tremendous change, reaches an all time high in recent times. The success of the institutes depends on the adaptability of the technology in the education. The quality in the institutes is connected to the effective utilization of information communication technology (ICT) methods in the institutes. Documentation and data management in the HEIs are the key areas in this direction. The recruiters are are looking for graduates from the accredited educational institutions. All the stakeholders are interested in these institutions. Though the institute accreditation is voluntary, there is a surge in approaching the accrediting councils for obtaining a better grade. In India, the accrediting authority is National Assessment and Accreditation Council (NAAC) and rankings are done by National Institutional Ranking Framework (NIRF). Higher Education Institutions (HEIs) need to understand the recent changes made in the NAAC, NIRF India Rankings process for achieving the better position in the ranking ladder. HEIs have to enrich the learning experiences of their students by providing them with state-of-the-art educational technologies. Facing the NAAC and NIRF is a mammoth and a challenging task that requires experts with in-depth knowledge of the higher education system in India. Research works, views, reviews and experiences of the experienced academicians and administrators are presented in this book.

The authors present their experiences and interpretations of Higher Education systems by providing global perspectives on the issues and challenges. Suggestions for the improvement of rankings in their institutes are also mentioned. Some of the authors are experienced NAAC assessors. The importance of life skills, ethical values and their integration into the curriculum is highlighted in this book. The idea of the book is to help the readers to cope with the changed scenario in bringing academic excellence of HEI. Quality of teaching, student's perceptions, teaching performance indicators are reviewed. The central theme in this volume is to analyze the new trends in HEI through the lens of ICT usage.

The authors and editors are greatly indebted to University Grants Commission (UGC) for its financial support through Government College for Women, Autonomous grants. I profusely thank Principal, Government College for Women (Autonomous) for hosting the National Conference through which the book project is made possible. I wish the discussions presented in this book open up new collaborations in emerging areas of education research. I hope that the students and academicians would be largely benefited from this book.

Sankara Narayana Rao Gedala
Department of Physics
Goverment College for Women Autonomous Srikakulam
Dr. B.R. Ambedkar University
Srikakulam, A.P.
India

List of Contributors

A. Ramarao	Department of Economics, Goverment Degree College, Tekkali, Dr. B.R. Ambedkar University Srikakulam, Tekkali, Srikakulam Dist, Andhra Pradesh, India
B. Preethi	Government College for Women (Autonomous), Srikakulam, Dr. B.R. Ambedkar University, Srikakulam, Andhra Pradesh, India
B.V.A.N.S.S. Prabhakar Rao	School of Computer Science and Engineering, Vellore Institute of Technology, Chennai, Tamil Nadu, India
Balvinder Shukla	Professor of Entrepreneurship, Leadership & IT, Amity University, Uttar Pradesh, India
Don Passey	Professor of Technology Enhanced Learning, Lancaster University, Lancaster, United Kingdom
F. Abid	Department of Telugu, Government College for Women Autonomous Srikakulam, Dr. B.R. Ambedkar University, Srikakulam, India
G. Sankaranarayana Rao	Department of Physics, Goverment College for Women Autonomous Srikakulam, Dr. B.R. Ambedkar University, Srikakulam, India
Godavari Venkata Murali Mohan	Department of Telugu, Government College for Women Autonomous Srikakulam, Dr. B.R. Ambedkar University, Srikakulam, India
K. Chakrapati	Department of Economics, Goverment Degree College Pathapatnam, Srikakulam, Dr. B.R. Ambedkar University, Srikakulam, India
K. Mythili	Goverment College for Women (A) Srikakulam, Dr. B.R. Ambedkar University, Srikakulam, India
K. Suryachandra Rao	Principal Goverment Degree College Pathapatnam Srikakulam, India
Karri Rama Rao	Department of Zoology, Goverment Degree College, Tekkali, Srikakulam Dt. Dr. B.R. Ambedkar University, Srikakulam, Andhra Pradesh, India
M.J.A. Swaroop	GITAM University, Visakhapatnam, India
M.R. Joginaidu	Department of History & Tourism, Goverment College for Women (A) Srikakulam, Dr. B.R. Ambedkar University, Srikakulam, Brazil
M.R. Jyothifrederick	Goverment Degree College, Narasannapeta, Srikakulam, Dr. Ambedkar University, Srikakulam, India
N.V.S. Bhagavan	Department of Physics, Government Degree College Men, Srikakulam, Andhra Pradesh, India
P.L. Saranya	Department of Physics, Government College for Women (Autonomous), Srikakulam, Dr. B.R. Ambedkar University, Srikakulam, Andhra Pradesh, India
Pradeep Kumar	Amity Institute of Information Technology, Amity University, Uttar Pradesh, India
Pulakhandam Srinivasa Rao	Gayatri College of Science and Management Srikakulam, Dr. B.R. Ambedkar University, Srikakulam, Andhra Pradesh, India
Smt. M. Santhi	Deptartment of Economics, Govt. College for Women (A) Srikakulam, Dr. Ambedkar University, Srikakulam, India

Smt. R.S. Goldina	Department of Chemistry, Government College for Women (Autonomous) Srikakulam, Dr. B.R. Ambedkar University, Srikakulam, India
Smt. T. Adilakshmi	Deptartment of Economics, Govt. College for Women (A) Srikakulam, Dr. Ambedkar University, Srikakulam, India
Smt. T. Kasiratnam	Department of Physics, Government College for Women (Autonomous) Srikakulam, Dr. B.R. Ambedkar University, Srikakulam, India
Sreeramulu K.	Goverment College for Women (Autonomous) Srikakulam, Dr. B.R. Ambedkar University, Srikakulam, India
Srinivasa Babu Ampalam	Gayatri College of Science and Management Srikakulam, Dr. B.R. Ambedkar University, Srikakulam, Andhra Pradesh, India

CHAPTER 1

Challenges of Higher Education Institutions in Assessment Accreditation and Ranking Framework Methodologies

K. Sreeramulu[1,*]

[1] *Goverment College for Women (Autonomous) Srikakulam, Dr. B.R. Ambedkar University, Srikakulam, India*

Abstract: The difficulties faced by the higher education institutions in the process of accreditation and rankings are presented in this chapter with reference to the Indian context. The performance of higher education in India is critically examined in the context of global standards. The main impediments are observed through various committee reports, and possible suggestions are discussed. The initiatives from the Government of India are noted in this chapter. It is observed that the second and third rated institutes are suffering most in the maintenance of quality benchmarks. It is found that the documentation of all academic activities in the digital form is not properly done. Need-based courses and interdisciplinary programs that cater to the requirements of the local and regional community are important for the creation of employment opportunities. Inadequate financial support and a large number of teaching vacancies are the major concern for the institutes in maintaining global standards. Assessment and Accreditation of Institutions are compulsory for all the institutions, and institutes are encouraged to participate in the National Institute Ranking Framework (NIRF) rankings. It is suggested to take into account the second-grade institutes' ideas and practices when they are available with a time stamp.

Keywords: Digitization, Documentation, Employment opportunities, GER, HRD, Human resources, Institute of excellence, Institute repositories, NAAC, NIRF, Premier institutes, Private university, Public university, Quality benchmarks, Research institutes, Timestamp, UGC, World rankings.

INTRODUCTION

In the post-independence scenario, being a democratic country, politicians give high priority to higher education in India. Under the headship of Pandit Jawaharlal Nehru and Abul Kalam Azad, the higher education system underwent great

---

* **Corresponding author K. Sreeramulu:** Goverment College for Women (Autonomous) Srikakulam, Dr. B.R. Ambedkar University, Srikakulam, India; Tel: 994 052 1011; E-mail: dr.ksreeramulu@gmail.com

transformation till 1980. After that, the education ministry introduced the Human Resources Development Department (HRD) under the central government wing. With the continuous efforts of HRD, the quality of higher education is improved, and it has introduced a number of wings to check the quality of higher education institutes (Basant, 2014). India is the third-largest country in the world with good quality of English speaking people compared to China. America and China stood first and second, respectively, in students' enrollment in higher education. The higher education system is governed by UGC, which not only monitors the standards of the institution but also provides financial assistance under different heads. India is providing higher education through IIT, NIT, Central and state universities, and deemed and private universities. Along with the above-said institutions, a number of scientific laboratories such as IISC, CSIR, ICMR, BARC, ISI economic research institutes, *etc.*, are contributing a lot to the higher education system in India. Due to various reasons, the Indian premier institutes have not been found in any place of the world university rankings.

There is also a proposal to award the Institute of excellence to some of the Indian institutes that produced high-impact on research-industry collaboration, which in turn creates job potential. These measures have also not brought reasonable positions in the global rankings (Agrawal,2006). On one side, the institutes are not able to attract the other country students, and on the other side, there is a lack of sports participation. The quality and quantity of research publications is another factor for the low performance in the global academic scenario. Even the premier institutes could not get financial support from the alumni for the development of the institutes. Often the institutes fail to understand the local job opportunity skills. In order to resolve the above-said problems, the universities, as well as, autonomous colleges should redesign their syllabus as per the requirement of employable opportunities. The outgoing student records should be well maintained, and the institutes use their services continuously so that alumni become strong in all aspects. For the achievement of the above-said goals, administrative support should be given to the faculty from the state and central governments. Highly qualified faculty should be recruited with the prescribed procedures in the institutes.

The financial support from the government is continuously increasing since independence, in terms of GDP 0.51 in 1951 to 4% in 2011. These figures are far below the global standards; Brazil 30% in 2011 (Reddy K.S., 2016). The institutes are making good progress both in research and academics, even with this low allocation of GDP. But the physical and academic infrastructure facilities are not sufficient to compete with the world-class institutes (Meyer, 2006). The institute repositories have not been correctly maintained, and the lack of correct academic information is one of the factors that the other country students have not joined these institutes. The institutes do not have any funds for the maintenance of facilities, and hence global standards could not be reached. The key positions like vice-chancellors, *etc.*, are left vacant quite often. These problems are to be addressed for the improved performance of the institutes in India. Regulatory bodies in all academic categories supervise the functioning of the institutes and offer suggestions for their quality enhancement. But this monitoring is not being done digitally and with human intervention. The problems crop up these methods. The present higher education sector in India needs a critical examination through digital procedures to meet the global standards. The government has recognized this lacuna and increased the budget allocations (Reddy, K.S., 2016). The Government of India, under the HRD has taken new initiatives in the accreditation procedures and ranking methodologies to evaluate the quality of the institutes through third party digital resources. In India, the National Assessment and Accreditation Council awards grades based on the performance broadly on Teaching Learning, Research, Extension activities, *etc*. Evolution is entirely based on digital verification and validation procedures for authenticity and acceptance globally. National Institutional Ranking Framework Methodology NIRF issues ranks entirely based on digital records.

The major challenge for both the center and state governments are providing the right amount of financial resources to the institutes. The private sector is also encouraged to establish institutes for filling the gap of world-class institutes. Creating competition between public and private institutes paves the path for the stakeholders to choose the institute of their choice.

CHALLENGES OF THE PRESENT HIGHER EDUCATIONAL SYSTEM IN INDIA-SUGGESTIONS

The present policies adopted in the higher education sector are not in tune with the requirements of contemporary society. The globalization of education poses new threats in the gross enrollment ratio in Indian institutes. The colleges are not able to attract the students from other countries. Interdisciplinary courses, twinning programs and programs with field based experience needs to be introduced in the universities to improve the students job opportunities. A new emphasis is to be given on courses coupled with community based programs and social issues. A systematic approach is to be adopted to introduce need based courses. The poor physical and academic infrastructure, lack of research publications, large number of teaching vacancies are some of the problems in the higher education system. accessibility of higher education to all sections of society.

Research in higher education is very low. Colleges in rural areas are facing a lot of problems, poor infrastructure, underrated students, under qualified teachers. The Government of India is taking all necessary steps for removing all obstacles in the way of development and instructed the regulatory bodies to coordinate the efforts of the institutes. All the institutes are encouraged to maintain their own digital data bases of all academic activities and adopt ICT based learning.

Industry and Academia Connection

It is necessary to have a collaboration between industry and academia. Internship training should be made available to the students in the local industries. The colleges situated in the rural and far off places are unable to get the industry internships. Virtual internships are an answer to this problem. More budget allocations to the education sector is the need of the hour. Diversified approach is to be adopted for rural and urban institutes to reach the quality benchmarks.

Incentives to Teachers and Researchers

Teachers with quality research publication are to be encouraged with incentives. Independent Regulatory Authority for Higher Education (IRAHE) is to be established to check the quality of higher education in India (Abramo, G, 2015). Number of universities is also to be increased.

Action Plan for Quality Improvement

In all the monitoring procedures, the records are to be verified digitally. Digitization of entire records is suggested. All the academic activities are to be placed in institute repositories with a time stamp. The institutes are expected to maintain the records with self explanatory and should be verifiable digitally. Effective utilization of available resources is to be followed by the institutes and this also should be subjected to digital verification. A separate academic dean is to be appointed to look after the financial support and management. Reasonable fee structure is to be followed by the institutes and this should be checked by the regulatory bodies (Abramo, G., 2015).

Student-Centered Education and Dynamic Methods

Participation in all academic and extracurricular activities and better time management is a big challenge in the semester system for the students as well as teachers. In the rural and semi urban areas, innovative methods are to be followed for the curriculum delivery to reach average and below average students. Students may take up social activities and join student organizations. The colleges may ensure that their social activities should not affect their learning performance. New methods are to be adopted to address this issue. Participation in local rural professions should also be recognized and due credits may be given by formulating new procedures. Personal counseling, students participation in seminars, organizing college events by students may be given importance in the colleges.

Student exchange, networking with other colleges and retaining their regional and local culture, tradition, are necessary for holistic development. The research in humanities and social sciences need to be relevant to contemporary society. Major share of the research publications are from the premier institutes like IIT, IIM and National laboratories. The contribution from state universities and colleges are meager.

Status of Academic Research Studies: The researchers per million population in Japan 5287 and US has 4484 whereas In India it is only 119. The number of doctorate degrees awarded per year is far below the global average (Gruber, 2014, Liu, 2015).

Need Based Job-Oriented Courses

There are diversified needs in different regions and the institutes should cater to satisfy the requirements through their new courses. These courses need not be data science or software related but are specific to the local and regional needs. This is one way to create a job potential in tune to the local or area development. The survey reports, case studies and research learning are to be focused to develop these models in a structured manner. In the developing countries the policy makers should concentrate in creating jobs in the rural areas also by work from home in the areas of data science related courses. Integration of local and regional jobs to the cloud services would meet the real purpose of creating large job potential. The students in the rural areas may be trained in cloud architecture to hire their services from their home. The holistic development of the human being is the need of the hour as the ethical and human values are most important in making a nation.

Holistic Development

Creativity and nativity is essential for personality development. The development of any country depends on the capacity of its purchase power parity. As India is a big market place because of its population the production and consumption of goods can be made possible by encouraging nativity and creativity. The personality built up by the individual is more helpful to get a place for him in the global market. The colleges and universities should create facilities for innovations, entrepreneurship and start ups. These practices should be duly recognized by Accreditation and Ranking Framework Organization. Many of the ideas generated in the rural and semi urban institutes are often taken into account with the local enterprising organizations. But this was not recognized by the accrediting organizations as it is not fitting into their framework. The institutes are encouraged to record the ideas put forth by the students or teachers digitally within a time stamp.

Accreditation and Rankings

All the stakeholders have a role in the college feedback process. Alumni, Recruiters are not showing keen interest to provide feedback on the institutes. Sometimes they are not even available to the rural colleges. In that case Philanthropists and the general public should be included in the feedback process at all colleges. Nowadays, students do not frequently walk into the libraries and refer to a printed book and the college libraries are already facing financial crunch in adding new books and journals. The national digital libraries like shodhsindhu and shodhganga *etc.*, are not being utilized effectively by the students. Awareness campaigns about the digital libraries are to be conducted by the colleges to the students and teachers and workshops are to be organized for effective utilization of their smartphone in reading the e-books. The assessment of the institutes broadly based on teaching learning, Research and extension activities. The NIRF 2017 has made it mandatory for all participating institutions to upload the data (submitted to the NIRF) on their websites besides making the same available on the NIRF's website in summary form. This transparency has added to NIRF's credibility. Most of the information is in numbers that allows easy computation once a methodology has been chosen. In the future interdisciplinary courses need more to get employment.

CONCLUSION

The reasons for lagging in the world rankings of the Universities are discussed. Documentation, industry collaborations, not recognizing the correct needs and problems of the local community not introducing the need-based courses are some of the problems faced by the institutes. Alumni support is not correctly tapped. The colleges are not tracking the students after the completion of their studies in the institutes. It is suggested that alumni enrollment may be made compulsory and is checked when they have joined in the jobs or at the time of getting financial support from the government for raising a startup. This would pave the way for strong alumni support for the institutes. Formulating a procedure of documenting the ideas and activities done by the rural and semi-urban colleges, which are the outside purview of present accreditation and ranking framework, is the need of the hour to bring them into rankings map.

CONSENT FOR PUBLICATION

Not applicable.

CONFLICT OF INTEREST

The author declares no conflict of interest, financial or otherwise.

ACKNOWLEDGEMENTS

Declared none.

REFERENCES

Abramo, G., D'Angelo, C.A. (2015). Evaluating university research: same performance indicator, different rankings. *J.Inf.*, *9*(3), 514-525.
[http://dx.doi.org/10.1016/j.joi.2015.04.002]

Agarwal, P. (2006). ICRIER Working Paper, Indian Council for Research on International Economic Relations Higher Education in India: The Need for Change. 180. http://www.icrier.org/pdf/ICRIER_WP180_Higher_Education_in_India_.pdf

Basant, R., Sen, G. (2014). Access to higher education in India: An exploration of its antecedents.
[http://dx.doi.org/10.2139/ssrn.2535644]

Gruber, T. (2014). Academic sell-out: how an obsession with metrics and rankings is damaging academia. *J. Mark. High. Educ.*, *24*(2), 165-177.
[http://dx.doi.org/10.1080/08841241.2014.970248]

Liu, W., Hu, G. (2015). China's global growth in social science research: uncovering evidence from bibliometric analyses of SSCI publications (1978-2013). *J. Inf.*, *9*(3), 555-569.
[http://dx.doi.org/10.1016/j.joi.2015.05.007]

Meyer, K.E. (2006). Asian management research needs more self-confidence. *Asia Pacific. Journal of Management*, *23*(2), 119-137.
[http://dx.doi.org/10.1007/s10490-006-7160-2]

Reddy, K. S., Qingqing Tang, EnXie (2016). Higher education; high-impact research, and world university rankings; a case of India and comparison with China. *Polit Sci Rev B: Human Soc Sci*, *2*(1), 1-21.
[http://dx.doi.org/10.1007/s10490-006-7160-2]

CHAPTER 2

Can a Student Feedback Provide Correct Opinion on Teaching-Learning Process in Higher Education Institutes?

G. Sankaranarayana Rao[1,*]

[1] *Department of Physics, Goverment College for Women Autonomous Srikakulam, Dr. B.R. Ambedkar University, Srikakulam, India*

Abstract: The relevance of student feedback to the quality of higher education institutes is highlighted in this chapter. Different student feedback formats and processes are reviewed. The importance of this process in enhancing the academic performance of the colleges is discussed in the Indian context. The popular feedback surveys are studied and their merits and drawbacks are mentioned. Student feedback data in electronic format is collected from a college in Andhra Pradesh, India, for 2019. The data is analyzed in light of the academic performance of the college. The study tries to find out whether the outcome of student feedback (SFB) provides the correct opinion of the students about the teaching-learning process of the higher education institutes (HEI). Results show that students have not given the true picture of teaching-learning of the institute. Possible reasons are discussed and suggestions are mentioned to make the SFB a relevant process in improving the academic grade and rank of HEI.

Keywords: College, Co-curricular, Employment, Extra-curricular, Grade, HEI, Higher education, ICT, IQAC, NAAC, Questionnaire, Rating scale, Skills, Student feedback, Student progression, Student, Survey, Teacher, Teaching-learning, University.

INTRODUCTION

National Assessment and accreditation council (NAAC) is the apex body to accredit the colleges and universities in India. The new NAAC procedures for the higher education institutes (HEI) pose a challenge in obtaining good grades and rank for the accredited and new institutes. Securing a better NAAC grade is a daunting task for the HEI in the changed scenario. The new NAAC methodology

---

* **Corresponding author G. Sankaranarayana Rao:** Department of Physics, Goverment College for Women Autonomous Srikakulam, Dr. B.R. Ambedkar University, Srikakulam, India; Tel: 944 1207 220; E-mail: anisotrop2y@gmail.com

Sankara Narayana Rao Gedala and P.L. Saranya (Eds)
All rights reserved-© 2021 Bentham Science Publishers

of quantitative, qualitative metrics, digital validation, and verification of the data demands the full utilization of information and communication technology (ICT).

Job oriented courses and skill development programs through Jawahar Knowledge center have been introduced. Digital and virtual classroom teaching, and online learning management systems are arranged in the colleges. Entrepreneurial, leadership, and soft skills classes have been taught as a part of the curriculum. Despite these efforts, lack of employability skills, low rate of student progression to higher education, poor campus placements are the main problems faced by the present HEI's in achieving good grades or rank. Students' opinion plays a key role in finding solutions to these problems (Abbot R.D., 1990).

The student feedback on teaching-learning experience in the classroom gave an insight into the difficulties experienced by the students. It paved the way for the teachers to use suitable methodologies for making learning an enjoyable experience.

Student evaluation through feedback is widely used in all colleges because of its ease and importance (Penny, 2003). It came into existence in the year 1970 (Galbraith, 2012). It is widely accepted that student feedback (SFB) is an important tool to find out the real reasons for the improvement of the college's academic performance (Ginns, P., 2007). It has been considered as an important part of the internal quality assurance cell (IQAC) in the institutes (Johnson, 2000). It is mostly used for formative as well as a summative evaluation of the institute (Arthur, 2009; Burden, 2008; Edström, 2008; Emery, Kramer, 2003). It is usually done once a year or semester. Students give their classroom experience through questionnaires (Little, 2010). The results are submitted to the head of the institute to adopt necessary changes of the teaching-learning process in tune with the student suggestions for improving the institute performance (Abrami, P. C., 1990). The teacher and students are integral parts of IQAC to build a quality culture (Harvey, 2003; Coates, 2005; Renée Stalmeijer, 2016; Jonas Flodén, 2017). The desirable characteristics for a good teacher are knowledge, communication skills, and competency in teaching. The research, teaching experience, and rank of the teacher are valuable indicators of a teacher. The SFB helps the teachers to know their weaknesses and strengths related to teaching-learning. Teachers consider feedback an important instrument in improving their teaching performance, and administrators also consider it in policy decisions.

There are many formats for SFB (Olivares, 2003; Ory, 2001; Onwuegbuzie, 2009). Open-ended, closed-ended and mixed methods. Students will take more time to answer open-ended questions, but opinions can be expressed in their own words. Closed-end questions are easy to complete, but opinion can not be given if they want to add any information. A mixed method with a suggestion section is the most common practice in all the colleges. Some of the popular surveys are Instructional Development and Effectiveness Assessment (Cashin, 1978), Students Evaluation of Teaching Effectiveness Rating Scale (Toland, 2005), the Student Course Experience Questionnaire (Ginns, 2007), and the Teaching Proficiency Item Pool (Barnes, 2008). The surveys must be economical (Braun, 2009), and their focus must be on effective teaching. Midpoint or neutral categories and scales are discussed by Onwuegbuzie (2009) in the survey questionnaire. Three types of scales: numbering, ranges, and the ordering of choices, are suggested by Sedlmeier in these feedback processes. All the stakeholders must be involved in the process of the survey separately. Student rating in the survey might not always represent actual learning, *e.g.,* students may fail the examination and still think that they have learned something.

Paper and electronic format questionnaire methods are followed in the institutes. Several studies made comparisons between these methods (Ling, T., 2012). Paper methods have certain defects. In this, the data collection is not done in real-time and could not be verified electronically. Students do not show interest in filling the questionnaire at the end of the semester. Most of the students are not available at that time. Often, they do not study the questions and copy answers from other students, and do not express their true feelings. The true perceptions of the students have not been found through conventional evaluation feedback (Brooman, 2014). Preservation of forms is another problem.

Most of the education institutes introduced an online student feedback system due to its accessibility and authenticity. Availability of (ICT) infrastructure and non-functioning of student emails are problems in this method. But the students can give feedback at their convenient time in this method.

The administrators and teachers would reshape their methods in accordance with the outcome of the feedback to improve the performance of the institute. Students' interest, their academic performance and socio-cultural background, and knowledge of the process play a vital role in obtaining the genuine outcome of the SFB process (Boring. A, 2016; Blair E, 2014; Brenda Little, 2010).

There are different opinions on the validity of student evaluation. Some faculty expressed fears about the use of SFB as the students do not show keen interest in giving feedback or marking the answers casually. Faculty members expressed apprehensions about the results of feedback as this can have serious implications on their career advancement. Students do not give correct opinions through feedback as they do not have proper orientation and knowledge (Aleamoni, 1999). Most of the research studies consider the survey results useful, but the apprehensions continue (Clayson, 2009). SFB is a key to the success of academic institutes. The policymakers and teachers would fine-tune their methods of pedagogy, student support services, and enhancement in employable skills. Often, the outcome of SFB does not represent their real aspirations and requirements.

The objective of the study is to find the SFB to give a clear picture of teaching-learning and whether the outcome matches the institute's academic performance, *i.e.*, graduation outcome, progression to higher education, and employment. The SFB data of a selected college in Andhra Pradesh is considered and analyzed in the study to examine the above research question. Students from arts, commerce, and science programs participated in a mixed-method (multiple choice and text-based) to give their feedback.

METHODOLOGY

Students submit the feedback by filling out an online questionnaire (google forms) after each course. Topics addressed in the questionnaire were: satisfaction with the teaching, encouragement towards co-curricular and extracurricular activity, depth teaching, follow-up, usage of ICT tools, career counseling, *etc*. The data is gathered and analyzed with a timestamp by a faculty-led program evaluation team. Students were asked to rate 20 statements on a five-point Likert scale, *i.e.*, 4 to 0, which embeds three categories of answers, *i.e.*, level of satisfaction, percentage of completion/implementation, and degree of impact, as shown in Table 1.

Table 1. Student Feedback Format.

Student Satisfaction Survey
Name of the College:
email:
Name of the Teacher:
Subject:
Semester/Year:
Instructions to fill the questionnaire:
All questions should be compulsorily attempted.
Each question has five responses, Choose the most appropriate one.
The response to the question No. 21 is an opportunity to give suggestions or improvements (Kindly restrict your responses to teaching learning process only).

Question	Your Response
1. How much of the syllabus was covered by the teacher?	-

(Table 1) cont.....

Question	Your Response
4- 85 to 100% 3- 70 to 84% 2- 55 to 69% 1- 30 to 54% 0- Below 30%	-
2. How well did your teacher prepare for the classes?	-
4- Thoroughly 3- Satisfactorily 2- Poorly 1- Indifferently 0- Won't teach at all	-
3. How well is the teacher able to communicate?	-
4- Always effective 3- Sometimes effective 2- Just satisfactorily 1- Generally ineffective 0- Very poor communication	-
4. The teacher's approach to teaching can best be described as	-
4- Excellent 3- Very good 2- Good 1- Fair 0- Poor	-
5. Frequency of the internal evaluation process by the teacher	-
4- Always Fair 3- Usually Fair 2- Sometimes unfair 1- Usually unfair 0- Unfair	-
6. Was your performance in assignments discussed with you?	-
4- Every time 3- Usually 2- Occasionally/sometimes 1- Rarely 0- Never	-
7. The teacher takes active interests in arranging field visits for students	-
4- Regularly 3- Often 2- Some times 1- Rarely 0- Never	-

(Table 1) cont.....

Question	Your Response
8. The teaching process in the classroom facilitates you in cognitive, social, and emotional growth	-
4- Significantly 3- Very well 2- Moderately 1- Marginally 0- Not at all	-
9. The teacher provides multiple opportunities to learn and grow	-
4- Strongly agree 3- Agree 2- Neutral 1- Disagree 0- Strongly disagree	-
10. The teacher informs you about expected competencies, course outcomes and program outcomes	-
4- Every time 3- Usually 2- Occasionally/sometimes 1- Rarely 0- Never	-
11. You does a necessary follow-up with an assigned task to you	-
4- Every time 3- Usually 2- Occasionally/sometimes 1- Rarely 0- Never	-
12. The teacher illustrates the concepts through examples and applications	-
4- Every time 3- Usually 2- Occasionally/sometimes 1- Rarely 0- Never	-
13. The teacher identifies your strengths and encourage you with providing the right level of challenges	-
4- Fully 3- Reasonably 2- Partially 1- Slightly 0- Unable to	-

(Table 1) cont.....

14. The teacher is able to identify your weaknesses and help you to overcome them	-
4- Every time 3- Usually 2- Occasionally/sometimes 1- Rarely 0- Never	-
15. The teacher makes an effort to engage students in the mentoring, review, and continuous quality improvement of the teaching-learning process	-
4- Strongly agree 3- Agree 2- Neutral 1- Disagree 0- Strongly disagree	-
16. The teacher uses the student-centric methods such as experiential learning and problem solving for enhancing learning experiences	-
4- To a great extent 3- Moderate 2- Somewhat 1- Very little 0- Not at all	-
17. The teacher encourages you to participate in extracurricular activities	-
4- Strongly agree 3- Agree 2- Neutral 1- Disagree 0- Strongly disagree	-
18. The efforts are made by the teacher to inculcate soft skills, life skills, and employability skills to make you ready for the world of work	-
4- To a great extent 3- Moderate 2- Somewhat 1- Very little 0- Not at all	-
19. The teacher uses ICT tools such as LCD projector, multimedia, *etc.*, while teaching	-
4- Above 90% 3- 70 to 89% 2- 50 to 69% 1- 30 to 49% 0- Below 29%	-
20. The overall quality of teaching-learning process in the class is very good	-
4- Strongly agree 3- Agree 2- Neutral 1- Disagree 0- Strongly disagree	-

21. Give three suggestions/observations to improve the overall teaching-learning experience in the class with reference to the teachers a) b) c)	

There is one open-ended question for more specific suggestions/observations. Submitted feedback on different teachers of the college is collected. The analysis is done on two levels (Cohen, P. A. 1981, Wright, S. L., 2012). The first one is calculated for college rating, and the second one is for individual faculty. College rating calculation is done by using Table **2**. The calculation is described as follows:

The total no. of feedback received to each question is N. Maximum score for each question is N x 4 =M. Here it is 1131x4 = 4524 (M). Different numbers of responses (n1,n2, n3, n4, n5) to each question of all the forms (all teachers) with different points on the scale are counted and posted, as given in Table 3. The same process is continued for all 20 questions. Total score is computed as n1x 4+n2x3+n3x2+n4x1+n5x0 = n. The rated score is obtained from (n/M) 4. Total No. of feedback to each faculty received are collected for the calculation of faculty rating. More than 20 feedback responses are received for some faculty and less number to other faculty. Feedback analysis is limited to 20 by random sampling method; if the number is less than 20, all the received forms are used. The same method of computation is followed for each question, and grading is given to each question. The single grade is given as per the median method, Table **5**.

Table 2. Student Feedback analysis Format.

Name of the College:
Subject:
Semester/Year:
No. of feedback responses received to each question with different points on 0 to 4 point scale, nil responses, total score and normalized points for the year XXXX.

S.No.	Question	4	3	2	1	0	Nil	Points
1	How much of the syllabus was covered by the teacher?	-	-	-	-	-	-	-
2	How well did your teacher prepare for the classes?	-	-	-	-	-	-	-
3	How well is the teacher able to communicate?	-	-	-	-	-	-	-
4	The teacher's approach to teaching can best be described as	-	-	-	-	-	-	-
5	Frequency of the internal evaluation process by the teacher	-	-	-	-	-	-	-
6	Was your performance in assignments discussed with you?	-	-	-	-	-	-	-
7	The teacher takes active interests in arranging field visits for students	-	-	-	-	-	-	-

(Table 2) cont.....

S.No.	Question	4	3	2	1	0	Nil	Points
8	The teaching process in the classroom facilitates you in cognitive, social, and emotional growth	-	-	-	-	-	-	-
9	The teacher provides multiple opportunities to learn and grow	-	-	-	-	-	-	-
10	The teacher informs you about expected competencies, course outcomes and program outcomes	-	-	-	-	-	-	-
11	You does a necessary follow-up with an assigned task to you	-	-	-	-	-	-	-
12	The teacher illustrates the concepts through examples and applications	-	-	-	-	-	-	-
13	The teacher identifies your strengths and encourages you with providing the right level of challenges	-	-	-	-	-	-	-
14	The teacher is able to identify your weaknesses and help you to overcome them	-	-	-	-	-	-	-
15	The teacher makes an effort to engage students in the mentoring, review, and continuous quality improvement of the teaching-learning process	-	-	-	-	-	-	-
16	The teacher uses the student-centric methods such as experiential learning and problem solving for enhancing learning experiences	-	-	-	-	-	-	-
17	The teacher encourages you to participate in extracurricular activities	-	-	-	-	-	-	-
18	The efforts are made by the teacher to inculcate soft skills, life skills, and employability skills to make you ready for the world of work	-	-	-	-	-	-	-
19	The teacher uses ICT tools such as LCD projector, multimedia, *etc.*, while teaching	-	-	-	-	-	-	-
20	The overall quality of teaching-learning process in the class is very good	-	-	-	-	-	-	-
21	Give three suggestions/observations to improve the overall teaching-learning experience in the class with reference to the teachers a) b) c)	-	-	-	-	-	-	-

Table 3. Feedback analysis of Government College for Women Srikakulam: No. of feedback responses received to each question with different points on 0 to 4 point scale, nil responses, total score, and normalized points for the year 2019.

S. No.	Question	4	3	2	1	0	Nil	Score	Points
1	How much of the syllabus was covered by the teacher?	983	93	14	12	0	29	4251	3.76
2	How well did your teacher prepare for the classes?	909	177	13	32	0	0	4225	3.74
3	How well is the teacher able to communicate?	878	202	20	2	0	29	4160	3.68
4	The teachers approach to teaching can best be described as	833	243	17	4	0	34	4099	3.62
5	Frequency of the internal evaluation process by the teacher	850	223	24	1	0	33	4118	3.64
6	Was your performance in assignments discussed with you?	847	226	22	3	0	33	4113	3.64

(Table 3) cont.....

S. No.	Question	4	3	2	1	0	Nil	Score	Points
7	The teacher takes active interests in arranging field visits for students	683	773	36	5	3	31	3928	3.47
8	The teaching process in the classroom facilitates you in cognitive, social, and emotional growth	805	264	26	5	0	31	4069	3.60
9	The teacher provides multiple opportunities to learn and grow	851	227	17	2	0	34	4121	3.64
10	The teacher informs you about expected competencies, course outcomes and program outcomes	797	279	20	2	0	33	4067	3.60
11	Your teacher does a necessary followup with an assigned task to you	828	244	28	1	0	30	4101	3.63
12	The teacher illustrates the concepts through examples and applications	879	197	19	1	1	34	4145	3.67
13	The teacher identifies your strengths and encourages you with providing the right level of challenges.	875	199	23	0	0	34	4143	3.66
14	The teacher is able to identify your weaknesses and help you to overcome them	805	259	29	4	1	33	4053	3.59
15	The teacher makes efforts to engage students in the mentoring, review, and continuous quality improvement of the teaching-learning process	855	220	25	1	0	30	4131	3.65
16	The teacher uses the student-centric methods, such as experiential learning, and problem-solving, for enhancing learning experiences	828	247	25	1	0	30	4104	3.63
17	The teacher encourages you to participate in extra curricular activities	815	258	25	3	0	30	4087	3.61
18	The efforts are made by the teacher to inculcate soft skills, life skills, and employability skills to make you ready for the world of work	811	267	21	1	0	31	4088	3.61
19	The teacher uses ICT tools such as LCD projector, multimedia, *etc.*, while teaching	689	319	66	7	18	32	3852	3.41
20	The overall quality of teaching-learning process in the class is very good	908	175	18	0	0	30	4193	3.71
21	Give three suggestions/observations to improve the overall teaching learning experience in the class with reference to the teachers Main suggestions: 1. ICT Usage 2.Digital class rooms 3.Computer Lab facilities 4. Communication lab facility 5. Field trips 6. Lab extra hours 7. conduct more tests 8. Loud voice	-	-	-	-	-	-	-	-

Table 4. Students participated in feedback 2019.

Discipline	No of Students Participated	Total Student Strength	Percentage of Participation
Science	340	620	55
Arts	39	247	16
Commerce	49	214	23
Total	428	1081	-

Table 5. Faculty grades in the year 2019.

Faculty	Points Calculated	Faculty	Points Calculated	Faculty	Points Calculated
XXX1	3.77	XXX15	3.6	XXX29	3.81
XXX2	3.66	XXX16	3.6	XXX30	3.52
XXX3	3.94	XXX17	3.87	XXX31	3.68
XXX4	3.62	XXX18	3.83	XXX32	3.82
XXX5	3.91	XXX19	3.8	XXX33	3.62
XXX6	3.31	XXX20	3.83	XXX34	3.55
XXX7	3.4	XXX21	3.81	XXX35	3.8
XXX8	3.4	XXX22	3.6	XXX36	3.62
XXX9	3.99	XXX23	3.6	XXX37	3.35
XXX10	4	XXX24	3.78	XXX38	3.6
XXX11	3.4	XXX25	3.68	XXX39	3.69
XXX12	3.4	XXX26	3.62	XXX40	3.65
XXX13	3.4	XXX27	3.53	XXX41	3.4
XXX14	3.87	XXX28	3.58	-	-

The study is performed at the Government College for Women, Srikakulam, Andhra Pradesh, India. The college falls under the accreditation of Dr. B. R. Ambedkar University Srikakulam. The research questions are 1) Whether the students evaluate the teaching-learning of the institute correctly. 2) Whether the institution's academic performance is in line with the SFB outcome.

RESULTS AND DISCUSSIONS

Student Feedback (SFB) data is collected for teaching learning experience in a selected college, Andhra Pradesh state, for the academic year 2018-2019. The college has 1029 Under Graduate (UG) students and 52 post graduate students (PG), (Table 4). There are 12 UG programs of 3 year duration and 3 PG programs of 2 year duration in the college and 428 students are participated in this feedback collection process. They have submitted 1131 electronic feedback forms. 55% science students, 16% arts students, and 23% commerce students participated in the feedback process as shown in Table **4** and Fig. (**1**). 178 students gave single feedback and 250 students gave multiple feedback.

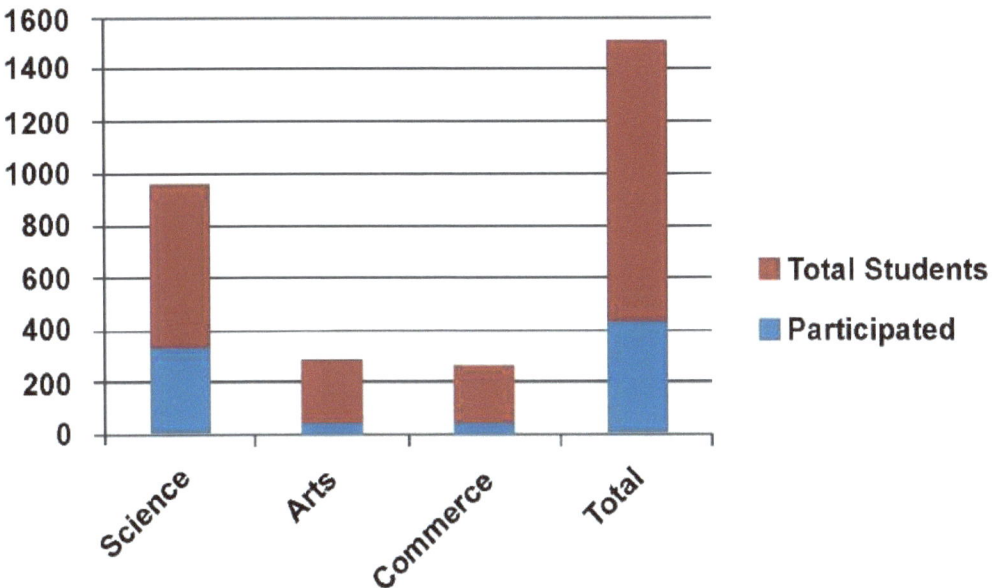

Fig. (1). Students participated in SFB among total strength in 2019.

Aggregate score to each question for entire faculty of College on 4 point scale is shown in Fig. (**2**) whereas individual faculty score given in Fig. (**3**). Students gave good rating to all questions except question number 7 and 19. It is observed that most of the students expressed field visits and ICT usage in the class room teaching are desirable. Many students stressed the need of ICT usage and digital class rooms in the text based question. The same was reported in earlier studies also (Harvey L, 2003). 811 responses out of 1131, *i.e.,* 72%, students gave highest rating to question number 18, related to employability skills. But it is learned from the college website students placements are 5%, progression to higher education is 30% graduation outcome is 70%. The placement statistics do not mach with the out come of the SFB.

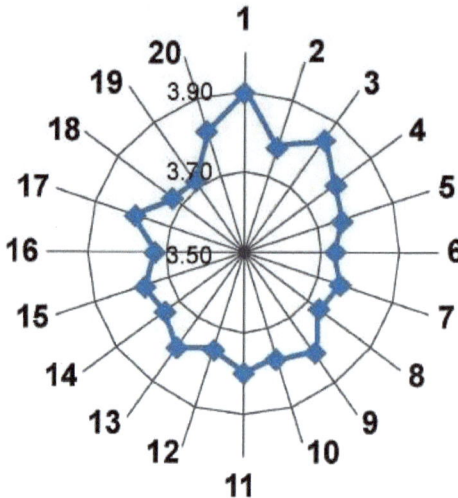

Fig. (2). College grade to each question for the academic year 2019-2020.

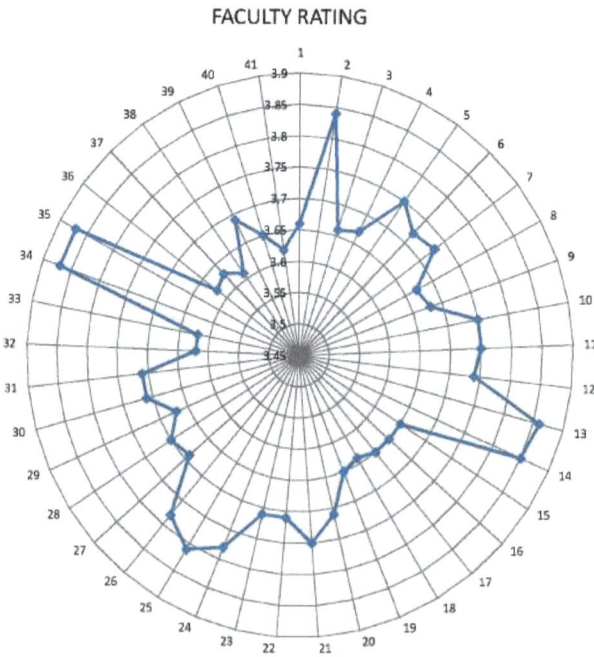

Fig. (3). Each faculty rating in teaching learning process for the year 2019-2020.

The mismatch is attributed to the following reasons. The rate of students participated in the survey affects the outcome (Nulty D. D., 2008). It is noted that students have not shown keen interest in answering the questionnaire. It is also reported by other studies (Dennis E. Clayson, 2018). They may not have proper knowledge about the questions in format (Diana Pereria, 2016). Student background characteristics also played an important role (Howard K. Wachtel 1998). The particular interest towards a teacher also affects the feedback (Mark Shevlin, 2000). Often students experience difficulty in expressing their true feelings about teachers because of the differential environment between student and teacher in a college. Students experience difficulty when given feedback on course coordinators, who award grades (Stalmeijer and de Grave 2008). All these factors affect the SFB.

The data analysis showed that SFB outcomes do not match with the institute's performance (Lizzio, A., 2002, Langbein, L., 2008). The true feelings of students could be found after conducting formal training on SFB (Spooren, P., 2013). Further research needs to look into better ways to involve the students in a meaningful manner in the SFB process in institutes of higher education. Student evaluation committees' participation in this process is also suggested (Renée Stalmeijer, *et al.* 2016).

Feedback from the stakeholders is an essential part of any academic institute in formulating their policies to improve institute performance. It is suggested to train the students to avoid casual answers in feedback 3). This would help the teachers and administrators to modify their methods and achieve a good grade in the accreditation procedures.

CONCLUDING REMARKS

An orientation program on the feedback process is desirable to both faculty, students, and administrators. Student evaluation committees may be formed for all academic activities of the institute. Separate feedback may be collected from these committees on teaching-learning activities, and this may be compared with the outcome of the feedback from general students. This would represent a real position of the academic institute.

CONSENT FOR PUBLICATION

Not applicable.

CONFLICT OF INTEREST

The author declares no conflict of interest, financial or otherwise.

ACKNOWLEDGEMENTS

Declared none.

REFERENCES

Abbott, R.D., Wulff, D.H., Nyquist, J.D., Ropp, V.A., Hess, C.W. (1990). Student opinions about instruction: The student perspective. *J. Educ. Psychol., 82*, 201-206.
[http://dx.doi.org/10.1037/0022-0663.82.2.201]

Abrami, P.C., D'Apollonia, S., Cohen, P.A. (1990). Validity of student ratings of instruction: What we know and what we do not. *J. Educ. Psychol., 82*, 219-231.
[http://dx.doi.org/10.1037/0022-0663.82.2.219]

Aleamoni, L.M. (1999). Student rating myths *versus* research facts from 1924 to 1998. *J. Person. Eval. Educ., 13*, 153-166.
[http://dx.doi.org/10.1023/A:1008168421283]

Arthur, L. (2009). From performativity to professionalism: Lecturer's responses to student feedback. *Teach. High. Educ., 14*, 441-454.
[http://dx.doi.org/10.1080/13562510903050228]

Ballantyne, R., Borthwick, J., Packer, J. (2000). Beyond student evaluation of teaching: Identifying and addressing academic staff development needs. *Assess. Eval. High. Educ., 25*, 221-236.
[http://dx.doi.org/10.1080/713611430]

Blair, E., Noel, K.V. (2014). Improving higher education practice through student evaluation systems: is the student voice being heard? *Assess. Eval. High. Educ., 39*(7), 10-16.
[http://dx.doi.org/10.1080/02602938.2013.875984]

Boring, A., Ottoboni, K., Stark, P. B. (2016). Student evaluations of teaching (mostly) do not measure teaching effectiveness. *Science Open Research*. https://www.scienceopen.com/document?vid=818d8ec0-5908-47d8-86b4-5dc38f04b23e
[http://dx.doi.org/10.14293/S2199-1006.1.SOR-EDU.AETBZC.v1]

Braun, E., Leidner, B. (2009). Academic course evaluation. Theoretical and empirical distinctions between self-rated gain in competences and satisfaction with teaching behavior. *Eur. Psychol., 14*, 297-306.
[http://dx.doi.org/10.1027/1016-9040.14.4.297]

Brooman, S., Darwent, S., Pimor, A. (2014). The student voice in higher education curriculum design: is there value in listening? *Innov. Educ. Teach. Int.*
[http://dx.doi.org/10.1080/14703297.2014.910128]

Burden, P. (2008). Does the end of semester evaluation forms represent a teacher's views of teaching in a tertiary education context in Japan? *Teach. Teach. Educ., 24*, 1463-1475.
[http://dx.doi.org/10.1016/j.tate.2007.11.012]

Cashin, W.E., Perrin, P.B. (1978). IDEA Technical Report No. 4. Description of IDEA Standard Form Data Base. *Manhattan, KS: Center for Faculty Evaluation and Development in Higher Education.* https://www.ideaedu.org/Portals/0/Uploads/Documents/IDEA%20Papers/IDEA%20Papers/PaperIDEA_50.pdf

Clayson, D.E. (2009). Student evaluations of teaching: Are they related to what students learn? A meta-analysis and review of the literature. *J. Mark. Educ., 31*, 16-30.
[http://dx.doi.org/10.1177/0273475308324086]

Clayson, D.E. (2018). Student evaluation of teaching and matters of reliability. *Assess. Eval. High. Educ., 43*(4), 666-681.
[http://dx.doi.org/10.1080/02602938.2017.1393495]

Coates, H. (2005). The value of student engagement for higher education quality assurance. *Qual. High.*

Educ., 11(1), 25-36.
[http://dx.doi.org/10.1080/13538320500074915]

Cohen, P.A. (1981). Student ratings of instruction and student achievement: A meta-analysis of multisection validity studies. *Rev. Educ. Res., 51*, 281-309.
[http://dx.doi.org/10.3102/00346543051003281]

Domen, Fernando (2006). Testing an instructional model in a university educational setting from the student's perspective. *Learn Instruct, 16*(5), 450-466.
[http://dx.doi.org/10.1016/j.learninstruc.2006.09.005]

Edström, K. (2008). Doing course evaluation as if learning matters most. *High. Educ. Res. Dev., 27*, 95-106.
[http://dx.doi.org/10.1080/07294360701805234]

Emery, C.R., Kramer, T.R., Tian, R. (2003). Return to academic standards: A critique of students' evaluations of teaching effectiveness. *Qual. Assur. Educ., 11*, 37-47.
[http://dx.doi.org/10.1108/09684880310462074]

Flodén, J. (2017). The impact of student feedback on teaching in higher education. *Assess. Eval. High. Educ., 42*(7), 1054-1068.
[http://dx.doi.org/10.1080/02602938.2016.1224997]

Galbraith, C., Merrill, G., Kline, D. (2012). Are student evaluations of teaching effectiveness valid for measuring student outcomes in business related classes? A neural network and Bayesian analyses. *Res. High. Educ., 53*, 353-374.
[http://dx.doi.org/10.1007/s11162-011-9229-0]

Ginns, P., Prosser, M., Barrie, S. (2007). Students' perceptions of teaching quality in higher education: The perspective of currently enrolled students. *Stud. High. Educ., 32*, 603-615.
[http://dx.doi.org/10.1080/03075070701573773]

Harvey, L. (2003). Student Feedback. *Qual. High. Educ., 9*(1), 3-20.
[http://dx.doi.org/10.1080/13538320308164]

Hoefer, P., Yurkiewicz, J., Byrne, J.C. (2012). The association between students' evaluation of teaching and grades. *Decis. Sci. J. Innovative Educ., 10*, 447-459.
[http://dx.doi.org/10.1111/j.1540-4609.2012.00345.x]

Johnson, R. (2000). The authority of the student evaluation questionnaire. *Teach. High. Educ., 5*, 419-434.
[http://dx.doi.org/10.1080/713699176]

Langbein, L. (2008). Management by results: Student evaluation of faculty teaching and the mis-measurement of performance. *Econ. Educ. Rev., 27*, 417-428.
[http://dx.doi.org/10.1016/j.econedurev.2006.12.003]

Ling, T., Phillips, J., Weihrich, S. (2012). Online evaluations *vs* in-class paper teaching evaluations: A paired comparison. *J. Acad. Business Educ., 12*, 150-161.

Little, B., Williams, R. (2010). Students' roles in maintaining quality and in enhancing learning: Is there a tension? *Qual. High. Educ., 16*(2), 115-127.
[http://dx.doi.org/10.1080/13538322.2010.485740]

Lizzio, A., Wilson, K., Simons, R. (2002). University students' perceptions of the learning environment and academic outcomes: Implications for theory and practice. *Stud. High. Educ., 27*, 27-52.
[http://dx.doi.org/10.1080/03075070120099359]

Nulty, D.D. (2008). The adequacy of response rates to online and paper surveys: What can be done? *Assess. Eval. High. Educ., 33*, 301-314.
[http://dx.doi.org/10.1080/02602930701293231]

Obergrise, Stefanie (2020). Students' emotions of enjoyment and boredom and their use of cognitive learning strategies – How do they affect one another? *Learn. Instruct., 66*, 101285. https://pred.uni-regensburg.de/id/eprint/44839/

Olivares, O.J. (2003). A conceptual and analytic critique of student ratings of teachers in the USA with implications for teacher effectiveness and student learning. *Teach. High. Educ., 8*, 233-245.
[http://dx.doi.org/10.1080/1356251032000052465]

Onwuegbuzie, A.J., Daniel, L.G., Collins, K.M.T. (2009). A meta-validation model for assessing the score-validity of student teaching evaluations. *Qual. Quant., 43*, 197-209.
[http://dx.doi.org/10.1007/s11135-007-9112-4]

Ory, J.C., Ryan, K. (2001). How do student ratings measure up to a new validity framework? *New Dir. Institut. Res., 109*, 27-44.
[http://dx.doi.org/10.1002/ir.2]

Pereria, D. (2016). Effectiveness and relevance of feedback in Higher Education: A study of undergraduate students. *Stud. Educ. Eval., 49*, 7-14.
[http://dx.doi.org/10.1016/j.stueduc.2016.03.004]

Shevlin, M., Banyard, P., Davies, M., Griffiths, M. (2000). The validity of student evaluation of teaching in higher education: love me, love my lectures? *Assess. Eval. High. Educ., 25*(4), 397-405.
[http://dx.doi.org/10.1080/713611436]

Stalmeijer, R., Whittingham, J., de Grave, W., Dolmans, D. (2016). Strengthening internal quality assurance processes: facilitating student evaluation committees to contribute. *Assess. Eval. High. Educ., 41*(1), 53-66.
[http://dx.doi.org/10.1080/02602938.2014.976760]

Sedlmeier, P. (2006). The role of scales in student ratings. *Learn. Instr., 16*, 401-415.
[http://dx.doi.org/10.1016/j.learninstruc.2006.09.002]

Spooren, P., Brockx, B., Mortelmans, D. (2013). On the validity of student evaluation of teaching: The state of the art. *Rev. Educ. Res., 83*, 598-642.
[http://dx.doi.org/10.3102/0034654313496870]

Stalmeijer, R., de Grave, W. (2008). De student als observator en feedbackgever voor docenten: een procesevaluatie [The Student and Observer and Feedback Provider for Teachers: A Process Evaluation]. *Tijdschrift Voor Medisch Onderwijs, 27*(5), 247-256.
[http://dx.doi.org/10.1007/BF03078281]

Toland, M., De Ayala, R.J. (2005). A multilevel factor analysis of students' evaluations of teaching. *Educ. Psychol. Meas., 65*, 272-296.
[http://dx.doi.org/10.1177/0013164404268667]

Wachtel, H.K. (1998). Student evaluation of college teaching effectiveness: a brief review. *Assess. Eval. High. Educ., 23*(2), 191-212.
[http://dx.doi.org/10.1080/0260293980230207]

Wright, S.L., Jenkins-Guarnieri, M.A. (2012). Student evaluations of teaching: Combining the meta-analyses and demonstrating further evidence for effective use. *Assess. Eval. High. Educ., 37*, 683-699.
[http://dx.doi.org/10.1080/02602938.2011.563279]

CHAPTER 3

A & A - Quantitative Metrics - A Bird's Eye View

K. Mythili[1,*]

[1] Goverment College for Women (A) Srikakulam, Dr. B.R. Ambedkar University, Srikakulam, India

Abstract: National Assessment and Accreditation Council (NAAC) has strived hard to safeguard and improve the academic standards and quality of higher education in India since 1995. In spite of 25 years of continuous monitoring and assessing the quality of education of HEI's and accreditation, the outcome is not encouraging with respect to the number of great institutions. This is high time that the gap is analyzed, and the lacunae between the assessment process by NAAC and the preparedness of institutions for assessment is identified. Based on the feedback received by NAAC over a long period, many changes have been made from time to time in the process of assessment. In July 2017, NAAC drastically revised the process for the HEIs. The new process represents an explicit paradigm shift, making it ICT enabled, objective, scalable and robust. Again very recently, on 17/12/2019, they have modified and published manuals for HEI's and reduced the number of metrics, both qualitative and quantitative. Though the new methodology is user friendly, an invisible lacuna has been observed that is evident from results. Many colleges which got A grade in the previous assessment have got B++ or B+ in this new methodology. In this scenario, an attempt is made to acquaint the stakeholders of the institutions regarding the overall A & A, in general, with a special emphasis on quantitative metrics, both essential and optional in particular. It also discusses in depth the basic problems facing the institution's preparedness.

Keywords: Accreditation, Assessment, CBCS, Emphasis, Environmental audit, Essential metrics, Feedback, HEIs, IQAC, IT infrastructure, Lacuna, Linkages, Mentoring, NAAC, New methodology, Optional metrics, Outcome, Qualitative metrics, Quantitative metrics, Recreation, Stakeholders.

INTRODUCTION

National Assessment and Accreditation Council (NAAC) has strived hard to safeguard and improve the academic standards and quality of higher education in India since 1995, through the process of assessment and accreditation of higher

---

[*] **Corresponding author K. Mythili:** Goverment College for Women (A) Srikakulam, Dr. B.R. Ambedkar University, Srikakulam, India; Tel: 9440520631; E-mail: pplmythili2007@gmail.com

Sankara Narayana Rao Gedala and P.L. Saranya (Eds)
All rights reserved-© 2021 Bentham Science Publishers

education institutions (HEI). Several institutions have gone through this process, and a sizable number have also undergone subsequent cycles of accreditation. Despite 25 years of continuous monitoring of the assessment of the quality of education of HEI's and accreditation, the outcome is not encouraging. NAAC identified 0.88% colleges as great institutions of higher learning(A++, A+ ; Based on 4500 assessed colleges) during 2005-2006.The great institutions increased to 2.6% only during Jan 2017-2020 (Based on 1473 Assessed colleges). Based on the feedback received by NAAC over a long period through eminent academicians, representing the universities and colleges sector and in tune with changing scenario of higher education, at the national and global level, NAAC has made many changes in the process of assessment and grading time to time.

NAAC introduced a new spirit into its process of assessment and accreditation in July 2017, and since then, the main focus of the revision process has been on the enhancement of the redeeming features of the accreditation process to make them more robust, objective, transparent, and scalable, as well as, ICT enabled (Rahul M. Mandal & Sanjay. D. Khiarnar 2018). It also has a reduced duration of the accreditation process. The process was shifted from qualitative peer judgment to data-based quantitative indicator evaluation with increased objectivity and transparency, extensive use of ICT, drastic reduction in the number of questions, size of the report, visit days, and so on, in terms of boosting bench-marking as a quality improvement tool. This has been attempted through introducing pre-qualifier for peer team visit, as 25% of system generated score, introducing System Generated Scores (SGS) with a combination of online evaluation (about 70%) and peer judgment (about 30%), and introducing the element of third party validation of data (NAAC Manual 2017). Though the new methodology is user friendly, an invisible lacuna was observed that was evident from the results. Many colleges which got A grade in the previous assessment got B++ or B+ in this new methodology. This is high time that the gap is analyzed, and the lacunae between the assessment process by NAAC and the institutions' preparedness for the assessment is identified. In this scenario, an attempt is made to acquaint the stakeholders of the institutions regarding the overall A & A, in general, with a special emphasis on quantitative metrics, both essential and optional in particular. The objective of this topic is to enlighten the concerned about the new methodology of assessment, to emphasize quantitative metrics, which have a major share in the assessment, and to caution the staff regarding the uploading of correct data to get good grading.

STUDY METHOD

The analysis mainly depends on secondary data such as self-study reports (SSR) of different HEIs, research papers on assessment, manuals published by NAAC from time to time, and observations made during HEIs visits as NAAC assessor.

NAAC Methodology and Challenges of HEI

Quantitative Metrics: NAAC has identified 121 metrics for affiliating colleges (qualitative metrics-42, quantitative metrics-79), and accordingly, they published manuals in July 2017. Later, on 17/12/2019, they slightly modified the metrics, and in the new method, they reduced metrics from 121 to 93, *i.e.*, qualitative metrics 35 and quantitative metrics 58 (NAAC Manual 2019). Accordingly, weightages for KI were also changed. One should take care of and keep in mind the weightages, which play a key role in grading while preparing the action plan of college activities, conducting activities, preparing documents year-wise, and presenting them meticulously in SSR and during the peer team visit. 70% of the evaluation was done on quantitative metrics online, and most of the institutions failed to present the data meticulously. Colleges are not performing suitable activities and not maintaining proper records in the prescribed format, IQAC not maintained by a single person continuously for 5 years, particularly in government colleges, the changing of the heads of the institutions frequently due to transfers, absence of proactive staff (both teaching and non-teaching), a large number of computer illiterates, particularly in rural areas, were the major reasons for the underperformance. Till today most of the undergraduate institutions have been restricted to conventional teaching methods only. not well suited to the concept of questions of 7 criteria. Hence an attempt is made to analyze some salient features of quantitative metrics criteria wise, so as to help the institutions to cope with the quality enhancement and quality sustenance activities.

Criterion I: Curricular Aspects

This criterion carries 100 weightage, among them 75 weightage for quantitative metrics (8 questions or metrics). This criterion emphasizes the curriculum-related issues like courses offered by the institution, introduction of new courses, conduction of add-on/value-added courses in the form of certificate/diploma courses, and syllabus with experiential learning and feedback on the syllabus from different stakeholders. Institutions, particularly of rural and semi-urban areas, are not able to conduct add-on courses in the true spirit due to lack of knowledge of KI, and often they are confused with terminology also. Add-on courses mean the courses which are introduced along with regular conventional courses, particularly for advanced learners(*ex*:- cyberlaw, GST, horticulture, *etc*.). Value-added courses are concerned with preparing the students to get placements in this competitive world and training the students in the form of short period courses, particularly for average and below-average students(*ex*:- spoken English, personality development, *etc*.). The certificate course period should be 6 months to one year with 16 credits or more than 30 teaching hours. The diploma course period should be 1 year to 2 years with 32 credits or more than 60 teaching hours. As per UGC guidelines, 95% of the universities have introduced the choice-based credit system (CBCS) system in their affiliating undergraduate colleges, where students have the flexibility to choose their courses from the lists of elective and core courses. In the syllabus, a board of studies (BOS) includes 3 or 4 clusters as electives. But due to workload problems and the non-availability of a sufficient number of teachers, only one elective is being taught for all students. Universities and governments should be concerned about these issues to enhance the quality of education. NAAC has more focus on experiential learning by the students through project works, field works, and internships. Most of the students are deprived of internships and research-based project works. NAAC expects feedback on the syllabus from all stakeholders, and most of the institutions are facing problems in this regard. Rural students are not in a position to identify lacuna in the syllabus. Academia-industry interactions are absent in most of the colleges. Hence getting feedback from employers does not arise. In some institutions, they collect feedback, but systematic analysis and action taken are not evident.

Criterion II- Teaching, Learning, and Evaluation

This criterion carries 350 weightage. Among them, 225 weightage is for quantitative metrics (9 questions or metrics). This criterion deals with the efforts of an institution to serve students of different backgrounds and abilities through effective teaching-learning experiences. It also probes into the adequacy, competence as well as continuous professional development of the faculty who handle the programs of the study. Most of the institutions may not have any problem uploading data with regard to most of the metrics as they deal with an enrollment of students, students admitted under reserved categories, student-teacher ratio, *etc*. Data regarding mentoring of students are not properly maintained by most of the institutions. Students are not aware of the latest technological developments, particularly in rural institutions. They need a good mentoring system for their holistic transformation. With regard to female students, it is more relevant, as 90% of them are anemic, suffering from the lack of proper toilet facilities, food of low nutritional value at social welfare hostels, early marriages, *etc*. Hence institutions must be ready to provide guidance, emotional support, and medical help when required through mentoring. Student satisfaction surveys also carry considerable weightage, so institutions should take care of this metric. They should train the students in such a way that they can face the online survey in a meticulous way.

Criterion III- Research, Innovations and Extension

This criterion carries 110 weightage, among them 100 weightage is for quantitative metric (10 questions or metrics). As more than 90% of the weightage was given to quantitative metrics, institutions should concentrate on these metrics for getting a good grade. This criterion deals with the facilities provided and efforts made by the institution to promote research culture and their outcome. Serving the community through extension and outreach programs is also a major concern of this criterion. Many of the colleges are not in a position to organize seminars/conferences at state and national levels. They do not properly understand that extension and outreach programs are very user friendly, if one can go through it thoroughly including data templates. It is easy to upload the information of metrics. However, most of the institutions open manuals at the end of 4th or 5th years of previous assessment. So there will be a huge gap between the available data and the data to be uploaded. In this regard the following points are worth remembering: (i) Seminars should be conducted for a specific topic with a small group of participants. (ii) Conferences are to be in large scale, with a specific subject with a larger group of participants. (iii) Workshops should be practicals oriented with a very small group of participants. They are also often confused about extension activities and outreach programs. Extension activities are categorized as curriculum related and community related activities. Curricular related activities are an extension of the learning process with some additional information, which include survey based project works, data collection of latest trends of a particular unit of a subject, preparation of flash cards, preparation of herbariums, collection of data of rare animals, chemical pollution of fruits and vegetables *etc*. (ii) Community related extension activities by and large include adoption of villages, health awareness programs, awareness on child marriages, blood donation camps *etc*., and they are carried out by NSS, NCC and WEC units of the college. Outreach programs are the activities that provide services to any population that might not otherwise have access to those services, which includes supply of competitive books to social welfare hostels, conducting of medical camps at tribal and hill areas, supply of first aid kits to the primary schools of rural and tribal areas, karyotype studies to mentally disabled children *etc*. Another important metrics of this criterion is data on linkages, collaborations,and MOUs of the institution for research, internships, project works *etc*. Most of the institutions are not able to get them, because of lack of awareness and and dearth of resources. They also get confused with all these terms and as a consequence provide inappropriate information. Linkage is nothing but an understanding between two, where one partner acts as a provider and another as a recipient. This may be between individual to individual or Institution to institution. Collaboration involves 2 or more parties but each and every one equally responsible for an outcome. MOU is having broader levels and a formal agreement between institutions with 2 or more firms for research, innovation and production. It involves financial aspects.

Criterion IV-Infrastructure and Learning Resources

This criterion carries 100 weightage, among them 71 weightage is for quantitative metrics (8 questions or metrics). This criterion emphasizes facilities available in an institution for maintaining quality of curricular and extracurricular activities. It also concerns the prospects of expansion of facilities for the future generations. NAAC also focuses on library facilities and IT infrastructure for academic and administrative purposes that are the needs of the hour. Most of the institutions do not have adequate IT infrastructure, hence students and staff are deprived of exposure to the latest developments and trends with respect to their subject. Many state governments improved to some extent, the IT facilities to their colleges by providing computers and other necessary equipment. Many of the staff members are not able to distinguish the different terminology of IT infrastructure leading to the wrong uploading of the information. LCDs are useful for the PowerPoint presentations by the staff, which impacts the learning capabilities of the students. Smart classrooms are furnished with computers, essential software, audience response technology, assertive listening devices, networking and audio/video capabilities. Learning management system (LMS) software is to deliver teaching and training online. Internet and Wi-Fi facilities are very important not only for classroom teaching, but also for organizing seminars and conferences.

Criterion V-Student Support and Progression

This criterion carries 140 weightage, among them 125 weightage is for quantitative metrics (11 questions or metrics). This criterion is very important in student point of view; highlighting the institution's assistance to the student community, to acquire the best experiences in learning, which are very important for their holistic development. Institutions should take care to conduct various sports and cultural events, encourage the students to participate in various inter collegiate competitions and involve them in various committees of the college, as all these factors carry a weightage of 50. Most of the institutions face problems in attracting campus drives and support from alumni.

Criterion VI-Governance, Leadership and Management

This criterion carries 100 weightage, among them 42 weightage is for quantitative metrics (6 questions or metrics). In this criterion, the weightage for quantitative metrics is less as compared to qualitative metrics. This criterion elicits the overall leadership calibre of the head of the institution through academic and financial management. Most of the colleges do not have any provision to support teachers in terms of giving financial aid to attend seminars/conferences. Empowered officials should concentrate on this point which is a very important factor of updating and sharing the knowledge of the teachers. Internal quality assurance cell (IQAC) is the heart of the institution and it has to pump the quality enhancement and quality sustenance measures to all the parts of the institution. The crucial role of IQAC is to prepare a plan of perspectives, organize all quality related curricular and co curricular activities, concentrate on documentation and submit annual quality assurance reports (AQAR) on time. The IQAC coordinator requires more autonomy, less workload of teaching, for better performance. In some institutions IQAC coordinators take charge without interest and work under pressure from the principal and management, as not many staff members come forward to assume charge as the coordinator.

Criterion VI-Institutional Values and Social Responsibilities

This criterion carries 100 weightage, among them 27 weightage is for quantitative metrics (6 questions or metrics). Weightage for quantitative metrics is too low as compared to all the other six criteria and carries only 2.7%. Most of the institutions fail to go for quality audits, which will inculcate environmental consciousness among staff and students. Green audit relates to the total area of the institution, land used for construction and data of fauna and flora of the institution. Energy audit relates to the total power consumption per year, use of LED lights and use of solar power. Environment audit includes green audit, energy audit, air quality, wastewater management, drinking water analysis, noise levels *etc*. All these audits are helpful to all stakeholders as they will be able to work in a congenial atmosphere.

Optional Metrics-Rules & Regulations

The provision is made for the HEI's to opt out from some of the metrics which may not be applicable to them for various reasons. Following are the rules for opting out from non applicable metrics: a) Maximum weightage of metrics that can be opted out from, should not exceed 30 (up to 3%). b) Metrics with maximum of total 10 weightage per criteria can only be opted out. c) All metrics in Criteria 1, 2 & 7 are essential. None of the metrics in these criteria can be opted out. d) Metrics identified as optional can only be opted out. e) Qualitative metrics cannot be opted out. The calculation of Cumulative Grade Point Average (CGPA) of Higher Education Institutions will be done excluding the metrics, opted out with 30 weightage (up to 3%) by the HEIs. This decision is aimed at helping HEIs, as they will not be assessed on metrics not applicable to them. HEIs willing to opt out from the non applicable metrics need to exercise the same, prior to final submission of SSR to NAAC.

A few important metrics of high weightage: 1) Student- Full time teacher ratio (20). 2) Average pass percentage of students during the last five years (30). 3) Online student satisfaction survey regarding teaching learning process, of about 20% students (60). 4) Number of extension and outreach programs conducted by the institution through NSS/NCC/Red cross/YRC *etc*.; (including the programs such as Swachh Bharat, AIDS awareness, gender issues *etc*., and/or those organized in collaboration with industry, community and NGOs), during the last five years (20). 5) Number of awards/medals for outstanding performance in sports/cultural activities at university/state/national/international levels (award for a team event should be counted as one), during the last five years (20). 6) Average number of sports and cultural events/competitions in which students of the institution have participated during last five years (organized by the institution/other institutions) (20).

The entire process of accreditation pivots on the core activity of teaching, learning and research. The teachers are expected to follow time lines for all the academic activities and engage the students both on curricular and extra curricular activities for the better outcome from the institution. All the quantitative and qualitative metrics require better outcome from the teaching and research activities. Better time management and choosing suitable metrics are the key for both the students and teachers in achieving the success of the institution.

The best way of choosing suitable quantitative metrics are explained. This helps the institutes in focusing on those metrics from the beginning of the academic year to achieve good grades in the assessment and accreditation procedures.

CONCLUSION

Lack of in-depth study of manuals by the head of the institution and other staff, lack of continuity in activities, not so good selection of activities, lack of perspective plan and proper documentation, and transfers of staff are some of the drawbacks. The financial problem, a big gap between sanction of works and execution of works (particularly govt-funded institutions), heterogeneous student community, ill-nourished female students and lesser number of permanent staff (both teaching and non-teaching) are some of the problems to be attended by the management to improve grading from one assessment to the other assessment by NAAC in future. For the last 4 months, the entire world is reeling under the impact of Covid-19, which has changed the lifestyles of people 360 degrees, and its impact would be felt by higher educational institutions also. Drastic changes will take place in the system, and academicians and policymakers have been busy with discussions regarding probable changes in higher education. The classroom teaching may be replaced by online teaching partially and seminars by webinars. Use of technology will be more in evidence, classroom structure may change, and examination pattern and evaluation process may too witness changes. The chances for conducting intercollegiate competitions are remote (at least 2 years), and there may be a drastic reduction in campus placements. In these circumstances, NAAC may come forward with few modifications in their assessment process.

CONSENT FOR PUBLICATION

Not applicable.

CONFLICT OF INTEREST

The author declares no conflict of interest, financial or otherwise.

ACKNOWLEDGEMENTS

Declared none.

REFERENCES

D.G. Sawant-2016-Role of IQAC in maintaining quality standards in teaching, learning and evaluation-pacific Science Review B. *Humanities and Social Science, 2*, 66-69.
[http://dx.doi.org/10.1016/j.psrb.2016.09.016]

M. Mandale, Rahul, D. Kairnar, Sanjay NAAC revised assessment and accreditation process at a glance. *IJTSRD, 2*(2), 271-277.
[http://dx.doi.org/10.31142/ijtsrd8391]

NAAC revised framework. (2017). http://www.naac.gov.in/

NAAC revised framework. (2019). http://www.naac.gov.in/

CHAPTER 4

Prominence of Student Support and Progression in the NAAC Assessment for Quality Augmentation in Higher Education Institutions of Andhra Pradesh India

Smt. T. Kasiratnam[1,*] and Smt. R.S. Goldina[2]

[1] *Department of Physics, Government College for Women (Autonomous) Srikakulam, Dr. B.R. Ambedkar University, Srikakulam, India*

[2] *Department of Chemistry, Government College for Women (Autonomous) Srikakulam, Dr. B.R. Ambedkar University, Srikakulam, India*

Abstract: In India, the quality and performance of its higher education institutes are continuously monitored by the University Grants Commission, the National Assessment and Accreditation Council, and the national institutional ranking framework. The universities are assessed and accredited based on seven criteria that carry 1000 marks. Out of the seven criteria, student support and progression have a 14% weightage for universities and autonomous colleges; for affiliated colleges, this is 10%, carrying 100 marks. This study considers the colleges in the Srikakulam district of Andhra Pradesh, where only one government college and two private colleges are accredited with an 'A' grade by the national assessment and accreditation council. The remaining institutes are yet to catch up to the quality benchmark and good grades. To achieve this, it is essential for all such institutes to improve their student support and progression performance. This chapter analyses the performance of such institutes and offers suggestions to improve their performance in the assessment process.

Keywords: Curriculum feedback, E-learning, Education system, Feedback analysis, Fifth criterion, Group learning, Higher education, Mentoring system, NAAC assessment, Placements, Prominence, Quality augmentation, Srikakulam, Student enrollment, Student support, Ward register.

INTRODUCTION

Established in 1994 as per the recommendations of the National Policy of Education 1986, the autonomous National Assessment and Accreditation Council

---

[*] **Corresponding author Smt. T. Kasiratnam:** Department of Physics, Government College for Women (Autonomous) Srikakulam, Dr. B.R. Ambedkar University, Srikakulam, India; Tel: 9550583364; E-mail: kasir8@gmail.com

Sankara Narayana Rao Gedala and P.L. Saranya (Eds)
All rights reserved-© 2021 Bentham Science Publishers

(NAAC) assesses and accredits higher education institutes (HEI) in India. Its headquarters is in Bangalore.

The NAAC accreditation's sub-structure is framed on five basic principles: (i) ameliorate national development, (ii) equip students with global competencies, (iii) instill in students a value system, (iv) encourage the use of technology, (v) pursuit transcendence. These five essentials form the bedrock for the assessment and accreditation of HEI by NAAC (P.S. Aithal et al., 2016). To calibrate educational institutions, the NAAC is authorized to give benchmarks. The NAAC letter grades and the cumulative grade point average (CGPA) are given in Table **1**. The assessment, as given in Table **2**, is based on seven criteria. This study focuses, in particular, on the fifth criterion: student support and progression. For institutes to get a good grade in the NAAC assessment process, they must consider and concentrate on this criterion. This criterion deals with several student-centered concepts. It has three sub-criteria: student support system, student progression, student's active role and participation. As per these criteria, teachers are expected to develop good relationships and nurture healthy interactions with students, all of which are crucial for students' academic as well as social development, mutual exchange of opinions, and development of trust towards teachers. In turn, this will further lead to strengthening the support system. Moreover, teachers can utilize the holiday period to interact with students through an e-learning system (NAAC Manual, 2018).

Table 1. NAAC letter grades and CGPA.

Range of Cumulative Grade Point Average (CGPA)	Letter Grade	Status
3.51 - 4.00	A++	Accredited
3.26 - 3.50	A+	Accredited
3.01 - 3.25	A	Accredited
2.76 - 3.00	B++	Accredited
2.51 - 2.75	B+	Accredited
2.01 - 2.50	B	Accredited
1.51 - 2.00	C	Accredited

Table 2. Different weightages of affiliated, autonomous colleges and universities as per NAAC manual 2018.

S. No.	NAAC Criterion	Affiliated Colleges	Autonomous Colleges	Universities
1	Curricular aspects	100	150	150

(Table 2) cont.....

S. No.	NAAC Criterion	Affiliated Colleges	Autonomous Colleges	Universities
2	Teaching-learning and evaluation	350	300	200
3	Research, consultancy and extension	110	150	250
4	Infrastructure and learning resources	100	100	100
5	Student support and progression	140	100	100
6	Governance, leadership, and management	100	100	100
7	Innovations and best practices	100	100	100

NAAC METHODOLOGY: STUDENT SUPPORT AND PROGRESSION

Student support system: In all government colleges and also some private colleges, student mentoring is practiced by offering student feedback. The mentoring process is continuously upgraded with suggestions from students. The feedback form consists of 20 questionnaires covering 100 marks. According to our analysis, all the government colleges are scrupulously maintaining the records manually and online every semester. This record is essential for institutes to attain a good national institutional ranking framework (NIRF) ranking and NAAC grading. All colleges are recommended to strictly maintain this record.

This record reveals students' satisfaction with the quality of teaching from different streams. Analyzing student feedback is essential as the institutional quality depends on students' point of view. Furthermore, it helps teachers make the necessary changes to their teaching methods and tailor them for students with various standards. The student feedback, questionnaires, group feedback, and student representation in consultative/scrutiny are analyzed and evaluated through the internal quality assessment and assurance cell (IQAC).

Curriculum Feedback

Curriculum feedback helps institutions and teachers better understand students' points of view, their areas of interest and offers a hint about the topics that need to be included in the subject. Because of the feedback, the syllabus can be modified accordingly and, thus, enable students to develop more interest in academics, which, in turn, helps them study at ease and excel in their studies. The feedback form, as shown in Table **3**, has 9 questions.

Maintenance of Ward Register

The ward register contains the entire profile of all students, their areas of interest, their parents' education, and occupation. It should be scrupulously maintained by the teachers. It helps them understand the diversity of the student population and motivates students as per their interests. It also helps the institutes in regularly monitoring the students regarding their participation in curricular and co-curricular activities.

Group Learning

In this kind of learning, students are divided into groups often led by the class's high-performing students. This helps students increase their CGPA and pass-out ratio. Moreover, in this system, the class mentors form e-groups, conduct quizzes and group discussions, and assign online assignments. Internal assessment is done based on this.

Table 3. Feedback form.

S.no	Question	Excellent%	Good%	Average%	Poor%
1	Depth of Syllabus content	-	-	-	-
2	Whether syllabus is career oriented	-	-	-	-
3	Interest generated by Teacher regarding syllabus is	-	-	-	-
4	How do you rate the sequence of units in the syllabus?	-	-	-	-
5	Rate the size of syllabus in terms of load on student	-	-	-	-
6	How do you rate the objectives stated and relevance to the course content	-	-	-	-
7	The internal evaluation system as it exists regarding syllabus is	-	-	-	-
8	What is your opinion about library holdings for the syllabus of your course?	-	-	-	-
9	Any suggestions	-	-	-	-

ANALYSIS: NAAC ASSESSMENT OF COLLEGES

The analysis was done by focusing on the various factors related to the fifth criterion of NAAC assessment in the colleges located in the urban, rural and tribal regions of the Srikakulam district. The data was obtained from Dr. B.R. Ambedkar University, Srikakulam. Student enrollment, it was found, increase in government degree colleges in all three regions, whereas such an increase is not observed in the private degree colleges located in tribal regions (Table **4**, Figs. **1** & **2**).

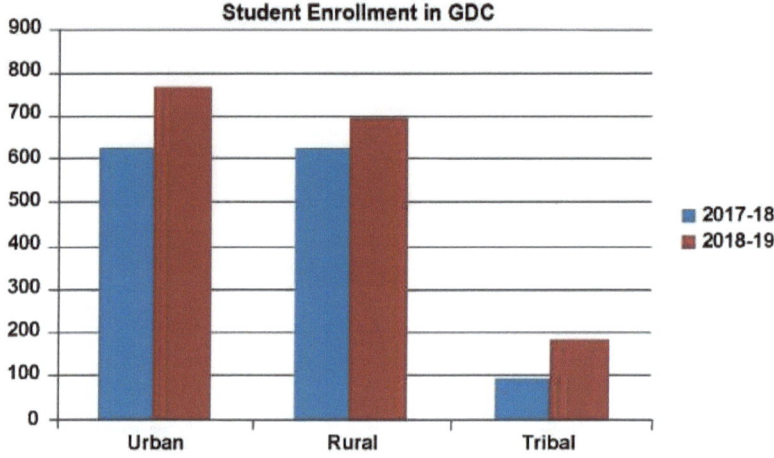

Fig. (1). The total enrollment of students in various regions in both government as well as private degree colleges is gradually increasing year-wise (during the academic years of 2017–18 and 2018–19).

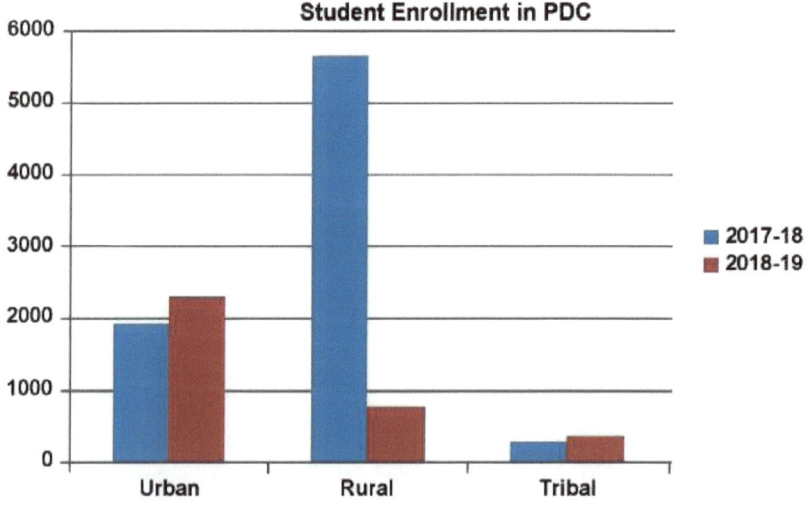

Fig. (2). Student enrollment in private degree colleges in the academic years 2017–18 and 2018–19.

Student Progression

The mercantile success of states is personally arbitrated by their education systems. Education is national strength (Younis Ahmad Sheikh *et al.*, 2017). The pass percentages in government and private colleges during the academic years 2017–18 and 2018–19 are shown in Fig. (**3**). It is more in urban and rural regions, whereas it is less in tribal regions. The performance of government colleges is better than private colleges.

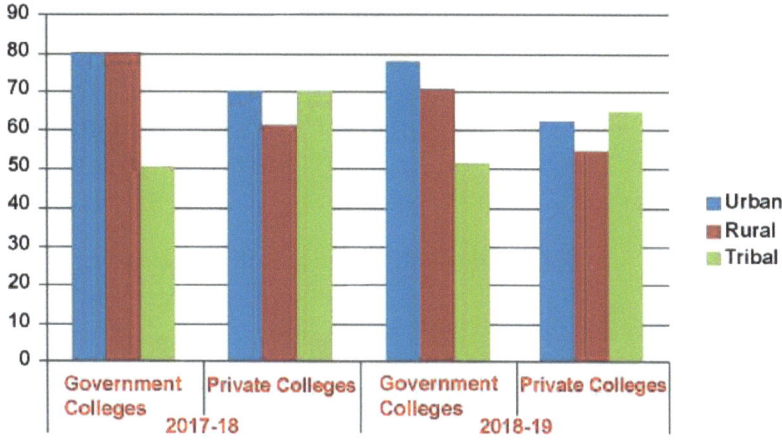

Fig. (3). Graduation outcomes of government degree colleges and private degree colleges.

Table 4. Enrollment ratios of students at graduation level in government and private degree colleges located in different areas for the academic years 2017–18 and 2018–19.

		Government Degree Colleges			Private Degree Colleges		
S.no	Academic Year	Urban	Rural	Tribal	Urban	Rural	Tribal
1	2017-18	626	622	92	1938	5664	266
2	2018 - 19	767	688	184	2284	7260	338

Table 5. Pass outs of government and private degree colleges of different areas for the academic years 2017–18 and 2018–19.

		Urban			Rural			Tribal		
Academic Year	Colleges	Appeared	Passed	%	Appeared	Passed	%	Appeared	Passed	%
2017-18	Govt.	626	501	80	622	495	79.5	92	46	50
	Private	1938	1359	70.12	5664	3459	61.4	266	186	69.9
2018-19	Govt.	767	597	77.8	688	484	70.3	184	95	51.6
	Private	2284	1428	62.5	7260	3984	54.8	338	220	65

Student Participation

This relates to the performance of students in a course outside their assessment. This includes class discussions, engagement in online discussions and student behavior in group activities, community services, and so on. Student participation will help them learn different skills. It will also help them learn from each other, which will increase their focus towards better understanding through cooperation. This, in turn, paves the way for mutual learning. These processes address the quality of teaching (Hernard, 2008).

Student participation in extracurricular activities would change their outlook towards the problems faced by society. As mentors, teachers play a big role in shaping the students' decisions when it comes to choosing employment or higher education. These practices largely help the institute in improving the academic performance of the institute.

The student-teacher ratio is low in all colleges in both the government and private sectors: it is around 1:60 in the science & commerce groups and 1:40 in art groups. Despite a low teacher–student ratio, the results are extremely good. The pass percentage is satisfactory in government and private colleges of urban areas, whereas in tribal areas, it is average. Though the government is providing necessary facilities to the students of tribal and rural areas through many schemes, they are not properly utilized due to the lack of parental perception of higher education.

It is essential for all the accrediting institutes to concentrate more on student support and progression. The data and analysis conducted by this study will be helpful for colleges in changing their strategies and securing a better place in the ranking framework.

CONCLUSION

In our analysis, it was observed that student enrollment has increased in government and private colleges in the urban and rural regions of the Srikakulam district. If they were given better mentoring along with a strong student support system, those colleges with a low NAAC grade and those colleges which are not yet accredited with a NAAC grading would have achieved a better ranking in the assessment process. As the enrollment of students is low in tribal regions, the number of government colleges with residential facilities in the tribal region should be increased. Mentoring also plays a decisive role in upgrading the enrollment ratio, graduation outcome, and progression to higher education and placements. It is a part of the fifth criteria in the NAAC assessment. The maintenance of a good mentoring system is essential in all colleges. Moreover, the college management in tribal areas has to make the necessary arrangements to include parental counseling as part of the mentoring system.

CONSENT FOR PUBLICATION

Not applicable.

CONFLICT OF INTEREST

The author declares no conflict of interest, financial or otherwise.

ACKNOWLEDGEMENTS

Declared none.

REFERENCES

Aithal, P.S., Shailashree, V.T., Suresh Kumar, P.M. (2016). Analysis of NAAC accreditation system using ABCD framework. *International Journal of Management, IT and Engineering,* 6(1), 30-44. file:///home/abhi/Documents/SSRN-id2779110.pdf

Henard, F. (2008). Report, learning our lesson: review of quality teaching in higher education. https://www.oecd.org/education/imhe/43961761.pdf

Sheikh, Y.A. (2017). Research scholar, higher education in India: challenges and opportunities MPISSR. *Ujjain Journal of Education and Practice,* 8(1), 2222-1735. https://files.eric.ed.gov/fulltext/ EJ1131773.pdf

CHAPTER 5

Higher Recompense to the Highly Qualified – A Way to Economic Development

P.L. Saranya[1,*], **N.V.S. Bhagavan**[2] **and B. Preethi**[3]

[1] *Department of Physics, Government College for Women (Autonomous), Srikakulam, Dr. B.R. Ambedkar University, Srikakulam, Andhra Pradesh, India*

[2] *Department of Physics, Government Degree College Men, Srikakulam, Andhra Pradesh, India*

[3] *Government College for Women (Autonomous), Srikakulam, Dr. B.R. Ambedkar University, Srikakulam, Andhra Pradesh, India*

Abstract: The economic growth of any country depends on its natural resources, human intellectual capital, progress in science and technology, and politically stable governments. Improper management of human and natural resources may be one of the key reasons for the underdevelopment. The financial deficit of a country precludes the offering of viable indemnity to the skill-oriented people, which causes brain drain. The brain drain theory is open-ended in developing countries. All the developed countries are utilizing the human intellectual resources of developing and underdeveloped countries. The human development index is low for the countries where human resource management is below par. Related statistics also indicate that low investment in higher education leads to low development in all aspects. All the developed countries spend a higher percentage of their gross domestic product on higher education. The quality and quantity of higher education institutions are the primary factors for development. Doctoral degree holders' salaries of different countries and their respective gross domestic products have been compared and analyzed in the light of the economic development in these countries. The structural changes that are required in the higher educational institutions for the holistic development of a country have also been suggested.

Keywords: Capacity, CSIR, Development, Economy, GDP, Gross enrollment, HDI, Higher compensation, Higher education, Industrial sector, Intellectual capacity, Quality, Service sector, Skill development, UGC, UNDP.

INTRODUCTION

An article published in the Economic Times on August 30, 2018, about the employment statistics in India was very astounding. It mentioned that 3,700 Ph.D.

---

[*] **Corresponding author P.L Saranya:** Government College for Women (Autonomous) Srikakulam, India; Tel: 9490764528; E-mail: lalithasaranyap@gmail.com

Sankara Narayana Rao Gedala and P.L. Saranya (Eds)
All rights reserved-© 2021 Bentham Science Publishers

holders, 50,000 graduates, and 28,000 postgraduates had applied for 62 posts of messengers in the Uttar Pradesh state police. The minimum eligibility required for that post was education till the fifth class. Recently in Andhra Pradesh, Dr. Aleem Basha Pinjari, a gold medalist and doctoral degree holder from the University of Hyderabad who had worked with Nobel laureate Ferrid Murad in the (United States of America) USA, was selected for the post of ward sanitary secretary. These instances indicate the status of higher education in India. About 16% of young men and 12% of young women in India are opting for tertiary qualifications. Persistent poverty might be a major reason for low enrollment in higher education institutes. Employment is the primary objective for these young men and women who seek to earn money for the fulfillment of their basic needs and those of their families. The University grants commission (UGC) and The Council for Scientific and Industrial Research (CSIR) do offer fellowships to talented students to enable them to pursue research careers. However, there has not been much progress in fundamental research in the country.

Students were forced by their poverty to opt for grade IV jobs. In India, 43.86% (2018 statistics) of the population is dependent on the agricultural sector for its employment. This sector does not require many qualified people. The industrial sector that requires technical and skill-oriented knowledge employs 24.69% of the population. The rest of the population, *i.e.,* 31.45%, works in the service sector.

Fig. (**1**) describes how HDI is a function of three major factors. These factors are life expectancy index, education index, and gross national income (GNI) purchasing power parity.

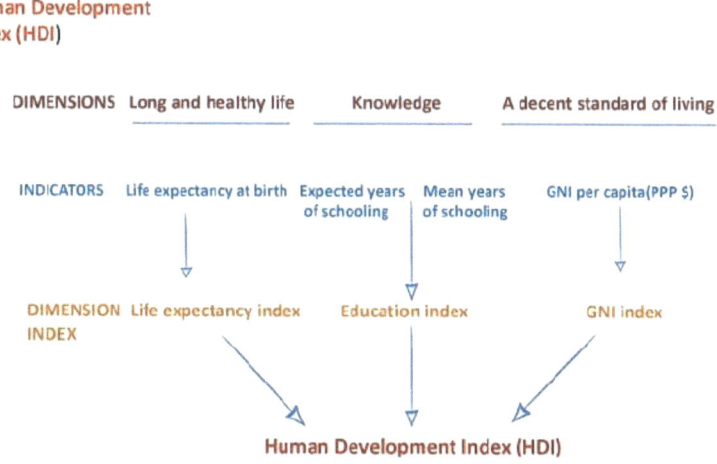

Fig. (1). United Nations Development Program's (UNDP) measures for the calculation of the Human Development Index (HDI).

All developed countries are investing more of their financial resources in health and education. The UNDP has placed India at the 135th place in the education index. The education index is very high (0.97) for Norway, which has also secured the top position on HDI.

GLOBAL TRENDS FOR INVESTMENTS IN INTELLECTUAL CAPITAL

It is important to retain highly qualified people, and this is the first step for the development of a country. The salaries drawn by Ph.D. holders in different sectors can be an important indicator for the retention of highly qualified people. In this study, the earning capacity of Ph.D. holders who are working in the higher education sector in different countries was examined and compared with different parameters such as HDI, per capita income, and GDP. All the developed countries are paying higher salaries to those members of their teaching communities who have achieved higher education levels, as shown in Table 1.

Table 1. Salaries paid to Ph.D. holders in different sectors.

Sector	USA ($)	India ($)
AGRICULTURE and NATURAL RESOURCES	79,000	14,000
ARCHITECTURE	78,000	17,000
ARTS	65,000	9,000
BUSINESS	1,02,000	20,000
COMMUNICATIONS and JOURNALISM	84,000	10,000
COMPUTERS and MATHEMATICS	90,000	18,000
CONSUMER SERVICES and INDUSTRIAL ARTS	94,000	20,000
EDUCATION	63,000	9,500
ENGINEERING	1,04,000	20,000
HEALTH	1,03,000	25,000
HUMANITIES and LIBERAL ARTS	99,000	24,000
LAW AND PUBLIC POLICY	89,000	24,000
PSYCHOLOGY and SOCIAL WORK	83,000	22,000
RECREATION	75,000	20,000
SCIENCE-LIFE/PHYSICAL	1,25,000	25,000
SOCIAL SCIENCE	1,05,000	15,000
STATISTICS	1,05,000	23,000
BIO-MEDICAL ENGINEERING	88,100	20,000

In all sectors, for the teachers, the maximum salary offered in the USA is $1,25,000, and the minimum salary is $65,000, whereas in India their salary ranges from $9,000 to $25,000, which is approximately seven times and five times higher in minimum and maximum values respectively for a highly qualified Ph.D. graduate. Around 30 developed, developing, and underdeveloped countries have been considered while conducting the present study. The salaries paid to assistant professors in all these countries were compared and are shown in Table 2.

Table 2. Salaries paid to Ph.D. holders in different countries.

S. No.	Country	Salary (USD/$)
1	South Africa	33,000
2	USA ($)	63,000
3	Germany	65,500
4	United Kingdom (UK)	74,000
5	India	9,500
6	Japan	64,000
7	Argentina	52,000
8	China	55,000
9	South Korea	36,000
10	Armenia	3,750
11	Saudi Arabia	45,000
12	Russia	7,800
13	Brazil	30,000
14	Australia	77,500
15	Canada	90,000
16	Mexico	21,500
17	Iran	20.000
18	Egypt	3,743
19	Venezuela	8,410
20	Pakistan	8,138
21	Turkey	27,934
22	Chile	35,900
23	France *(incl. overseas territories)*	58,150
24	Yemen	75,000
25	Thailand	13,000

(Table 2) cont.....

S. No.	Country	Salary (USD/$)
26	Spain	70,000
27	Sweden	54,630
28	Norway *(incl. overseas territories)*	63,780
29	Switzerland	1,44,860
30	Finland*(incl. Aland Islands)*	61,900
31	Italy	34,470
32	New Zealand	58,550

Higher Education in India

The higher education system in India is the largest, with a high number (~ 50,000) institutions of higher education. The first-generation students are more in India, and the social environment does not support a student being able to spend quality time on education. Consequently, the quality of education is relatively low, and this causes low employability. Although the gross enrollment ratio in higher education institutions is increasing consistently, the quality of higher education is yet to be improved. Even though research is a vital component in higher education, it receives less focus and attention in India. Teaching and conducting examinations alone cannot help achieve the overall development of the student. Some other opportunities are also required, such as industrial exposure to the students, minor projects, use of the learning-by-doing methodology, timely updates to the curriculum as required by the industry, *etc*.

Trow Martin (1976) studied higher education among elites between 1850 and 1950 and pointed to a broad consensus among educated persons on what knowledge was of utmost value and what qualities of mind and character should be possessed by an educated person. There are many "innovative" and "experimental" educational arrangements that offer a trivial and conventionally fashionable kind of education. Dorothee *et al*. reported the short-term effects of higher education on the labor market outcomes of highly skilled workers. They estimated the effect of improved quality of education on the employment prospects of university-trained individuals. They found that education reforms led to significant increases in the rate of employment.

A newspaper article by Celia W. Dugger, in The New York Times, stated educated workers were leaving poor nations. The exodus of skilled workers from poor countries is clearly a sign of a deep economic, social, and political problem in these countries.

A study had compared the compensations of higher degree holders with the compensation offered to various professionals in the field of higher education in the USA. Fig. (**2**) illustrates the compensation details for higher degree holders in different countries. It can be seen from this illustration that developed countries such as Switzerland, Canada, Australia, and the USA are offering higher salaries to highly qualified people, whereas Thailand, Pakistan, Venezuela, Egypt, Russia, Armenia, and India are offering a lesser salary to the intellectuals. This is the reason for intellectuals to migrate. The Indian government is investing low on high returns and high on low returns.

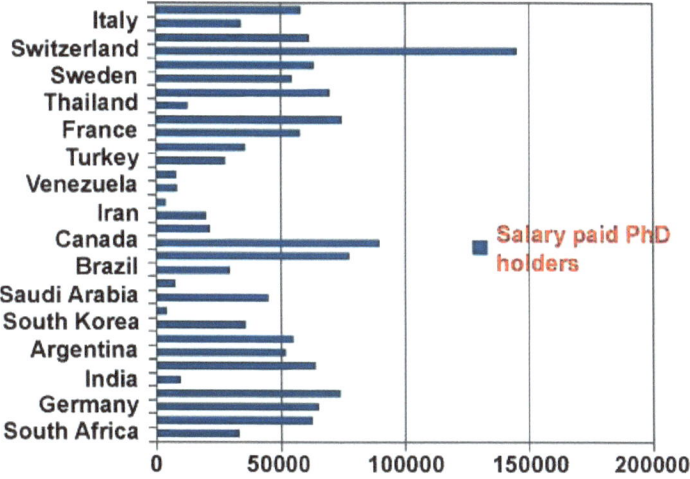

Fig. (2). Salaries of Ph.D. holders in various countries.

Fig. (**2**) represents the comparison of salaries paid in various sectors in the USA and India. It is clear that in all the sectors, India pays only 20% – 30% of the salary that could be earned in the USA. Hence, all the intellectuals are migrating to the countries where higher salaries are offered. Only the people of less intellectual capacity are staying in the country and rendering their services such that the outcomes of their efforts are low. The quality of education has declined due to migration.

Proposed Structural Changes in the Education System in India

Economically poor and intellectually strong students should be supported, notwithstanding their caste, sex, creed, race, and community, by providing additional facilities to them in institutions of higher education. The state and central governments should take the lead in this regard. The intellectual capacity of these students would be useful for the development of modern and sophisticated technology in various sectors. The intellectual capacity of economically poor students will also be useful in rendering good governance to the people of this nation in the government, public, and private sector companies. The authors are assuming a concept called intelligent investment on developing intellectual brains.

For this purpose, these authors propose the following model:

Conduct a common entrance examination throughout the country for admission into undergraduate programs – B.A., B.Sc, and B.Com. Based on the cream of the cream concept, 500 students should be selected from each district. These students should be provided college education, hostel facilities, free and hygienic food facility throughout the year, five sets of free uniform per annum, required set of free books for every year in each district headquarter itself. In addition to being provided these facilities, these students should be trained for admission into premier education institutions.

Suggested Learning Methodologies

Innovative teaching, learning methods are crucial for the development of student skills and subject understanding. The institutes are to be encouraged to introduce project-based, problem-solving-based learning methods. Project-based learning is a method centered on the learner. It allows for an in-depth investigation of a topic. In this kind of learning, the students go through an extended process of inquiry in response to a design question, a problem, or a challenge that usually requires more than individual efforts to handle and overcome. It is helpful for developing long-term learning skills to develop a deep, integrated understanding of content and process. Project-based learning also contributes to bringing the classroom close to the profession through the acquisition of knowledge while solving practical and real cases close to the professional world (Finlay and Faulkner). Problem-based learning assignments can be short, or they can be more involved and take a whole semester. It is often group-oriented. It is beneficial to set aside classroom time to prepare students to work in groups and to allow them to engage in their problem-based learning project (Duch *et al.*).

The Boyer Commission on Educating Undergraduates in the Research University (1998) suggests that a research university should create education to produce an individual "equipped with a spirit of inquiry and a zest for problem-solving." The National education goals panel (1992) similarly suggests that undergraduate education should be linked to producing definite outcomes, such as critical thinking, problem-solving, effective communication, and responsible citizenship. Similarly, the Wingspread report (1994) suggests that students should be able to think in complex ways, to analyze the information, to solve the problems.

Problem and project-based learning are not only applied to the core subjects but also to the fundamental courses like communication and soft skills (CSS). It is recognized that problem-based learning and project-based learning might be valid aims of any curriculum striving to become independent or autonomous (Roschelle & Teasley). It is suggested that problem-based learning and project-based learning enhance student knowledge and undergraduate program outcome. The curriculum is to be redesigned in such a way that the students are to be involved in community service for a semester period, and due credits are to be allotted for this purpose. Teachers are encouraged to train the students in the preparation of village and community survey reports and help them in identifying the local social problems and possible solutions. Delivering quality education and developing employability skills play a vital role in the ranking and accreditation procedures. This chapter emphasizes the methods of quality education to be inducted to the students of various social backgrounds.

CONCLUSION

In the current scenario of the above statistics, it is highly important to allocate certain high budgets to the higher education sector. Qualified people should be recognized in different categories, and they should be paid appreciable amounts according to their work. Quality human resources should be paid high on par with the developed countries. Countries like India are still following the conventional methods of rewarding talent and are not utilizing the available intellectual resources up to the mark. In the coming 4th industrial revolution period, compensation should be determined according to merit rather than on qualification or skills without qualification.

CONSENT FOR PUBLICATION

Not applicable.

CONFLICT OF INTEREST

The author declares no conflict of interest, financial or otherwise.

ACKNOWLEDGEMENTS

Declared none.

REFERENCES

Barbara, J.D. The power of problem based learning. *Sterling, VA Stylus.* https://styluspub.presswarehouse.com/ browse/book/9781579220372/The-Power-of-Problem-Based-Learning

Celia, W. Dugger newspaper article, newyork times, educated workers leaving poor nations, survey finds. https://www.nytimes.com/2005/10/26/health/study-finds-doctors-abandoning-poor-nations-for-rich-ones.html

Duch, B.J. (2015). Dorothée boccanfuso alexandre larouche mircea trandafir, quality of higher education and the labor marke in developing countries: evidence from an education reform in senegal IZA DP No. 9099. [http://dx.doi.org/10.1016/j.worlddev.2015.05.007]

Roschelle, J., Teasley, S.D. The construction of shared knowledge in collaborative problem. http://umdperg.pbworks.com/f/RoschelleTeasley1995OCR.pdf

Sara, J.F., Guy, F. Reading groups and peer learning. *Journal of Active Learning in Higher Education.* [http://dx.doi.org/10.1177%2F1469787405049945]

Trow, M. (1976). "Elite higher education": an endangered species? *Minerva, 14*(3), 355-376. [http://dx.doi.org/10.1007/BF01096277]

CHAPTER 6

Role of Digitization in Higher Educational Institutions for Better Ranking & Employability

B.V.A.N.S.S. Prabhakar Rao[1,*]

[1] School of Computer Science and Engineering, Vellore Institute of Technology, Chennai, Tamil Nadu, India

Abstract: The Higher Educational Institutions (HEIs) are to be transformed from paper-based hard copies to E-mode soft copies for data preparation, maintenance, and submission to any ranking agency. In this context, the digital platform is to be created for the distribution of information. Apart from that, government, aided, and private institutions have been facing many issues to transform the knowledge as per the stakeholder needs in terms of assessment criteria like curricular aspects, teaching-learning, and evaluation. Artificial intelligence (AI) is a buzzword in the higher education sector, as it is considered necessary to change the entire world's face, taking steps towards digitization. Smartphone usage by the student and teacher community is rapidly growing in all parts of the world. This research focuses on virtual connectivity through smart devices for better, effective results to beat the world competition. The extensive use of the smartphone for the right cause can help us in the right ways, such as in IPR notifications and preparatory documents for research publications in reputed journals and conferences, innovations through patent filing, and book publications. This proposed framework indicates how long and in what way students can equip themselves with the required skills. The present system recommends the overall evaluation category as exceptional, good, above average, or below average with parameters such as intellectual ability, maturity, perseverance, oral and written communication, analytical ability, imagination and creative ability to work with others, potential as a researcher, and self-confidence. Many semi-urban, rural, and agency teachers and students to date struggle due to not having the proper infrastructure or facilities for their education. Where there is a shortage of amenities such as teaching, library, and sports, AI technology can be handy. There is a huge amount of data being generated from different institutions and handling this amount of data using the RDBMS is very difficult. This is where big data comes into the picture. Big data is one of the key pillars of global digitization. By using big data, we can improve education quality and coordination and reduce maintenance costs. Predictive analytics and statistical tools and techniques can be used to improve student learning course outcomes.

---

[*] **Corresponding author B.V.A.N.S.S. Prabhakar Rao:** School of Computer Science and Engineering, Vellore Institute of Technology, Chennai, Tamil Nadu, India; Tel: 9952096275; E-mail: bvanssprabhakararao@gmail.com

Sankara Narayana Rao Gedala and P.L. Saranya (Eds)
All rights reserved-© 2021 Bentham Science Publishers

Keywords: Accreditation, AI, Analytics, Assessment, Big data, Computer, Decision making, Digitization, E-certificate, E-learning, E-registration, Employability, Gurukul, HEIs, Internet, Intelligence systems, Machine learning, Ranking, Social media, Sustainability, Technology.

INTRODUCTION

The role of HEIs is to provide public safety in an ethical manner with respect to social, economic, cultural, environmental, health, legal and sustainable factors. Everyone is well aware of the kind of system followed in ancient times to teach children. Moreover, the present-day education system is very different from it. An earlier form of the education system was known as the gurukul system. The education was more practical, and the child got to be more connected to nature. It contributed to the overall development of the child.

The present system is very different from the gurukul. A child receives an education in a school and spends certain hours there. He does not have to stay in school or perform any daily chores. Though digitization has many advantages in the field of education, due to the digital availability of all kinds, the dependency on teaching-learning online resource materials has drastically increased. The physical book-reading habit among the students has vanished, and referring to ebooks has become the norm. Excessive use of the internet and social networking sites is distracting students. They are now wasting most of their time scrolling on news feeds, memes, and status updates. Taking cognizance of the diversity in the kinds of institutions, HEIs have been grouped under three categories, namely, universities, autonomous colleges, and affiliated/constituent colleges. Leaving these aside, the most important thing is to receive knowledge. There are different teachers for different subjects that a child has to cope with. There is much more focus on theoretical knowledge gaining than practical training or implementation. Another crucial factor is that children have to study all subjects and cannot concentrate on their passion. Their curiosity is killed by studying all subjects and doing more theoretical work or appearing for tests and exams all the time. The purpose of educating our children is their overall growth and helping them to lead independent lives; it is not to produce mass workers to earn money or become machines.

MODERN METHODS – DELIVERY OF CONTENT

Digitization of academic activities in the institutes helps the teaching-learning process become fun and enjoyable for the students. Lecturers find it convenient to make the students well-informed before their actual class. Embedding employable skills into the core subjects is desirable for a progressive education system.

Digitization helps both the students and teachers save time and ensures that the skill teaching does not affect the core subject learning. The lecturers are expected to adopt various social media platforms for the knowledge transfer and evaluation of the students. Teachers can easily capture the attention of the students while the students can easily understand using the technology-based teaching aids and concepts. Students thus have more time to learn other employable skills that may interest them. Many educational applications are available on smartphones, which helps in improving the quality of the student's learning. Hence, there is a need to focus the students' ability on the digital infrastructure and learning resources and support their progression of originality, motivation, written and verbal comprehension and expression, and judgment. In many areas, the average educational qualification of a human being is moderate or poor due to some technical, administrative, social, or economic issues. In spite of their lifestyle, their direct contribution to society is as follows:

a) contribution to national and global income; b) supply chain of services; c) provision of surplus resources; d) shift of services; e) managing infrastructure; f) helping reduce inequality as per the dream of every nation; g) operative demand between public and other sectors; h) equal employment opportunities to rural and urban agencies; and i) unlimited wealth and health.

Any national/international governmental or non-governmental authorities/ organizations focus on assessment and accreditation to maintain the standards in the quality of education with respect to the global need. Agencies like NAAC, MHRD, ABET, and QS world ranking focus on the following aspects while assessing and accrediting the academic institutions: a) curricular – with respect to curriculum design and implementation; b) global reputations and ranking of the institution as per best practices; c) students pursuing higher education in the top institutions; d) student employability and package; f) alumni success rate – world famous/nobel laureates; g) teaching-learning and evaluation; h) research, innovations, and extension; i) infrastructure and learning resources; j) student support and progression; and k) governance, leadership, and management. Of course, the aspects may overlap or be duplicated in one or two areas but the key factors remain the same in the assessment and accreditation process.

LITERATURE REVIEW

The revolution of digitization has changed the way people think, behave, communicate, and earn their livelihood. The digital revolution is the new wave all around the world, including in India. The digital revolution is also called the third industrial revolution. Digitization is the beginning of the information era (Rao, 2020). The use of computers by teachers and students with the help of the internet has made it easier for digital communication and understanding customer's buying decisions (Rohan Samson, 2014). The viewpoints of various authors with respect to the paradigm shift in the mode of delivering content as per the present-day need of society is discussed in Table **1**.

Table 1. Role of digitization in HEIs.

S.No.	Author	HEIs – Viewpoint
1	Rohit Menon, 2014	Need for a Paradigm Shift
2	Rohan Samson, 2014	Digital Communication on Customer Buying Decision
3	Mohamed Sarrab, 2016	Software Quality Mobile learning services
4	Salih Rakap, 2016	Data extraction programs
5	Jessica Kornmann, 2016	Multi-perspective hypermedia environment
6	Naseem Hallajow, 2016	The interplay of technology Students' electronic literacy
7	Thuy Duong, 2016	Industry 4.0
8	Christoph Pimmer, 2016	Mobile and ubiquitous learning
9	Kriti Priya, 2017	Factors influencing Whistle Blowing Intentions of Teachers
10	Claudius Lieven, 2017	GIS-based system
11	Johnny Kwok, 2018	Digital Technology & FM
12	Vandana Ahuja, 2018	Quality Business School education and the expectations of the corporate
13	Mandie Scamell, 2018	Online story telling (SMEOLE) Online Learning Effectiveness
14	Clémence, 2018	Technology Change on Employment
15	Charlotte Wang, 2019	Sustainability Innovation in Universities, Digitization
16	Mark Murphy, 2019	Digital scholarship
17	Thuy Duong, 2019	Digitization – Job roles, skills & competence
18	Lydia Bals, 2019	PSM, & Current & Future Requirements
19	Eva Martínez-Caro, 2020	Digital Organization Culture
20	Diego Sinitò, 2020	I-PETER

PROPOSED SYSTEM

E-copy/soft copy maintenance – good quality of E-records – should be instituted. Student-centered learning with digitization is indispensable for any educational institute, as seen in Fig. (**1**).

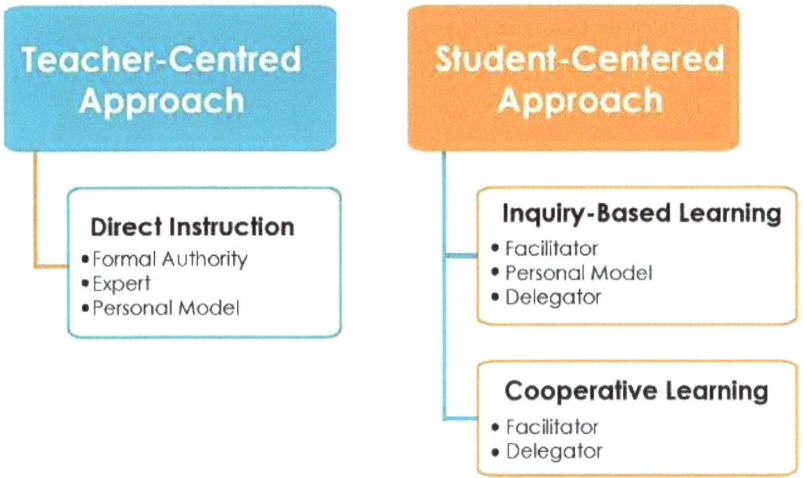

Fig. (1). Teacher-centered Learning *vs.* Student-centered Learning.

The following steps are proposed for the digitization of the institute to deliver content. Step 1 and 2 deal with the notification for admission and digitization of modern education, respectively. Step 3 is a virtual assistant – in the era of digitization, how can the education sector fall behind? The entire world is moving towards digitization in order to meet the present-day needs and India has to keep pace with it. The following apps are major sources for student's learning, as seen in Table **2**. The internet is one of the fundamental ideas of the development and advancement of digital technologies, and it has become a major source of education now. Instead of lectures in class and class assignments and homework at home, the classes are now flipped so that students can watch or listen to lectures at home and do assignments and homework in school (Table **2**). Step 4 is **E-records** – dealing with workforce prioritization, as seen in Table **3**. Step 5 is the validation of all academic and administrative databases through this process, as seen in Fig. (**5**). Step 6 is the assessment, which includes a scientific approach to achieve this task.

Table 2. Educational apps.

S.No.	Name of the App
1	BYJUS
2	UNACADMENY
3	TOPPR
4	BRAINER
5	GRADE UP

Table 3. E-Records for data retrieval and analysis.

R#	AI-based E-Records		
	Student Record	Traditional	AI Role
1	Student ID	Yes	Yes
2	Student Branch	Yes	Yes
3	Name of the Student	Yes	Yes
4	Parent Name	Yes	Yes
5	Age	Yes	Yes
6	Gender	Yes	Yes
7	Aadhar No.	Yes	Yes
8	Blood Group	Yes	Yes
9	Allergies if any	No	Yes
10	Special Care if any	No	Yes
11	Organization where working	No	Yes
12	In case of Emergency, Contact no	No	Yes
22	Insurance Type/Coverage	No	Yes
23	Health Card Details	No	Yes
24	Vehicle Type/Details	No	Yes
25	Other Support, if any	No	Yes

Step 7 is support regarding the use of mobile technology in education. Entering the present data and historical data slows down the process of dealing with actual facts. In many areas, the average educational qualification of a human being is moderate or poor due to any technical, administrative, social, or economic issues. The possible job opportunities are given in Table **4**.

Web-based information resources, telephone messaging – SMS or MMS – and the remote monitoring of student videoconferences are some methods to reach students. Step 8 is digital learning *via* important platforms on social media: Today, the internet is the gateway to limitless information about the future, past, and present. It is the podium where information is poured out from all possible mediums, and the students' feeds include everything. Social media is a medium where people express themselves openly, with or without their true identity, and the content they pour out is enormous. Here, we are trying to project only the pros of social media onto students. Let's begin with the eminent social media marketing platforms.

Table 4. Types of job opportunities.

Job Opportunities	Rural	Urban	Semi-Urban	Agency
Virtual Assistants	High	High	High	High
Translator	Low	Low	Low	Nil
Web Developer	Low	Low	Low	Low
Travel Agent	High	High	High	High
Freelance Writer	High	High	High	High
Social Media Manager	High	High	High	Nil
Data Entry	High	High	High	High
Call-Center Representative	Low	Low	Low	Nil
Blogging – Blogger	Low	Low	Low	Low

Table 5. Various social media sources for E-learning, teaching & research.

Methodology	Category	Usage
Facebook	Yes	Very High
Instagram	Yes	High
Twitter	Yes	Very High
Wikipedia	Yes	Very High
Linkedin	Yes	Moderate
Pinterest	Yes	Moderate
Online Assignment	Yes	Low
Virtual Classrooms	Yes	Very High
webinars Sessions	Yes	High
Urgent Homework Help	Yes	Very High
Assignment Writing Services	Yes	Very High
Online Dissertation Writing Services	Yes	Moderate
Google Hangout	Yes	Very High
Skype	Yes	Low
WhatsApp	Yes	Very High

Step 9 is teaching and monitoring in the digital classroom. Compassionate attention is very important in effectively dealing with students. Sympathy, empathy, altruism, concern, consideration, care, kindheartedness, respect, comfort are needed to improve one's holistic attitude. Step 10 is the intelligent system for HL7 records of the student and employee. With the help of technology, the system can maintain the HL7 records. Step 11 is getting in touch with us *via* phone – leaving a voice-mail or communicating *via* WhatsApp, Skype, *etc*.

The importance of ICT usage in the documentation and delivery of the teaching-learning process and other administrative records must be highlighted. The effective use of digitization gives institutes the necessary fillip to enhance their performance in accreditation and ranking.

CONCLUSION

This chapter has comprehensively described the methods and tools in the present education system and has also discussed the ways to improve the mode of delivering content in an effective manner. Of course, a large number of methods and tools are present; however, there are still several important challenges left unattended. The present education system is in the digital era. This digitization helps the education system on many fronts: teaching, learning, evaluation, research, and publications. The locations of educational institutes and the sources of knowledge have become immaterial due to the internet facilities and online resources. The time of teaching-learning has no importance in the digital era. But at the same time, the emotional intelligence of the teachers and students has deteriorated to such an extent that the dignity of student-teacher relationships has been lost. Therefore, many stakeholders of the education system have expressed their views on digitization. Though digitization has many advantages in the education system, the important traditional teaching skills of the teachers and the values learned in the schools and colleges cannot be replaced.

CONSENT FOR PUBLICATION

Not applicable.

CONFLICT OF INTEREST

The author declares no conflict of interest, financial or otherwise.

ACKNOWLEDGEMENTS

Declared none.

REFERENCES

Ahuja, V., Purankar, S. (2018). Quality Business School education and the expectations of the corporate-A research agenda. *Procedia Comput. Sci., 139*, 561-569.
[http://dx.doi.org/10.1016/j.procs.2018.10.209]

Aubert-Tarby, C., Escobar, O.R., Rayna, T. (2018). The impact of technological change on employment: The case of press digitisation. *Technol. Forecast. Soc. Change, 128*, 36-45.

[http://dx.doi.org/10.1016/j.techfore.2017.10.015]

Bals, L., Schulze, H., Kelly, S., Stek, K. (2019). Purchasing and supply management (PSM) competencies: Current and future requirements. *J. Purchasing Supply Manage.*, *25*(5), 100572.
[http://dx.doi.org/10.1016/j.pursup.2019.100572]

Gupta, K.P., Chaudhary, N.S. (2017). Prioritizing the factors influencing whistle blowing intentions of teachers in higher education institutes in India. *Procedia Comput. Sci.*, *122*, 25-32.
[http://dx.doi.org/10.1016/j.procs.2017.11.337]

Hallajow, N. The interplay of technology and context in Syrian university students' electronic literacy practices, Computers in human behavior. *Journal of Computers in Human Behavior. Part A.*
[http://dx.doi.org/10.1016/j.chb.2015.08.050]

Johnny, K.W.W., Ge, J., He, S.X. (2018). Digitisation in facilities management: A literature review and future research directions. *Autom. Construct.*, *92*, 312-326.
[http://dx.doi.org/10.1016/j.autcon.2018.04.006]

Kornmann, J., Kammerer, Y., Anjewierden, A., Zettler, I., Trautwein, U., Gerjets, P. (2016). *How children navigate a multiperspective hypermedia environment: The role of spatial working memory capacity, Computers in Human Behavior.* Part A.
[http://dx.doi.org/10.1016/j.chb.2015.08.054]

Lieven, C. (2017). DIPAS - Towards an integrated GIS-based system for civic participation. *Procedia Comput. Sci.*, *112*, 2473-2485.
[http://dx.doi.org/10.1016/j.procs.2017.08.182]

Martínez-Caro, E., Cegarra-Navarro, J.G., Alfonso-Ruiz, F.J. (2020). Digital technologies and firm performance: The role of digital organisational culture. *Technol. Forecast. Soc. Change,* *154*, 119962.
[http://dx.doi.org/10.1016/j.techfore.2020.119962]

Menon, R., Tiwari, A., Chhabra, A., Singh, D. (2014). Study on the higher education in India and the need for a paradigm shift. *Procedia Econ. Finance,* *11*, 866-871.
[http://dx.doi.org/10.1016/S2212-5671(14)00250-0]

Murphy, M., Costa, C. (2019). Digital scholarship, higher education and the future of the public intellectual. *Futures,* *111*, 205-212.
[http://dx.doi.org/10.1016/j.futures.2018.04.011]

Oesterreich, T.D., Teuteberg, F. (2016). Understanding the implications of digitisation and automation in the context of Industry 4.0: A triangulation approach and elements of a research agenda for the construction industry. *Comput. Ind.,* *83*, 121-139.
[http://dx.doi.org/10.1016/j.compind.2016.09.006]

Oesterreich, T.D., Teuteberg, F., Bensberg, F., Buscher, G. (2019). The controlling profession in the digital age: Understanding the impact of digitisation on the controller's job roles, skills and competences. *Int. J. Account. Inf. Syst.,* *35*, , 100432..
[http://dx.doi.org/10.1016/j.accinf.2019.100432]

Pimmer, C., Mateescu, M., Gröhbiel, U. (2016). Mobile and ubiquitous learning in higher education settings. A systematic review of empirical studies. *Comput. Human Behav.,* *63*, 490-501.
[http://dx.doi.org/10.1016/j.chb.2016.05.057]

Rakap, S., Rakap, S., Evran, D., Cig, O. (2016). *Comparative evaluation of the reliability and validity of three data extraction programs: UnGraph, GraphClick, and DigitizeIt, Computers in Human Behavior.* Part A.
[http://dx.doi.org/10.1016/j.chb.2015.09.008]

Rao, (2020). Disruptive Intelligent System in Engineering Education for Sustainable Development. *Procedia Comput. Sci.,* *172*, 1059-1065.
[http://dx.doi.org/10.1016/j.procs.2020.05.155]

Samson, R., Mehta, M., Chandani, A. (2014). Impact of online digital communication on customer buying

decision. *Procedia Econ. Finance, 11*, 872-880.
[http://dx.doi.org/10.1016/S2212-5671(14)00251-2]

Sarrab, M., Elbasir, M., Alnaeli, S. (2016). *Towards a quality model of technical aspects for mobile learning services: An empirical investigation, computers in human behavior.* Part A.
[http://dx.doi.org/10.1016/j.chb.2015.09.003]

Scamell, M., Hanley, T. (2018). Midwifery education and technology enhanced learning: Evaluating online story telling in preregistration midwifery education. *Nurse Educ. Today, 62*, 112-117.
[http://dx.doi.org/10.1016/j.nedt.2017.11.036] [PMID: 29316460]

Sinitò, D., Fugazzotto, M., Stroscio, A., Coccato, A., Allegra, D., Barone, G., Mazzoleni, P., Stanco, F. (2020). I-PETER (Interactive platform to experience tours and education on the rocks): A virtual system for the understanding and dissemination of mineralogical-petrographic science. *Pattern Recognit. Lett., 131*, 85-90.
[http://dx.doi.org/10.1016/j.patrec.2019.12.002]

CHAPTER 7

Education "Re" Creation

M.R. Joginaidu[1] and M.J.A. Swaroop[2,*]

[1] *Department of History & Tourism, Goverment College for Women (A) Srikakulam, Dr. B.R. Ambedkar University, Srikakulam, India*

[2] *GITAM University, Visakhapatnam, India*

Abstract: Human beings are one of the earth's creations that looks around their problems and think about their responsibility to find a solution and take action accordingly. In nature, every creature except human beings is playing its role to make the world beautiful. You will know the difference if you imagine the earth with and without human beings. As per the world economic forum 2018 report, no less than 54% of all employees will require significant improvement in skills by 2022. By observing our present situations and demands, we can predict that this is the time to prove the worth of our existence in nature by making the world beautiful. The education system is the only possible solution that makes the world beautiful by enabling people to have a good mindset. This study is used to assess the challenges and solutions for reshaping the future of education. Innate abilities, natural ways of learning, inner programming, and new ways of learning are used to reshape the future of education according to the psychological aspect of a human being and student needs. To discover our talents, we need to follow a framework/process which gives us the freedom to blossom. The need of the hour is to design a new framework for reshaping the future of education. In the future, we, as people of the nation, have the responsibility to create an environment in which each student could naturally study for recreation.

Keywords: ASER, Decision making, Innate abilities, Inner programming, Mission, Modern technology, NIEPA, Passion, PISA, Play-based education, Practical knowledge, Psychological aspect, Purpose, Recreation, Schooling, Self-chosen activities, Theoretical knowledge, Traditional wisdom, Work-life balance.

INTRODUCTION

A country that does not have its education in place lags everywhere. The same thing is happening in our country. Knowledge is one of the factors that differentiates us from other living organisms. Education is our passport to the

---

[*] **Corresponding author M.J.A. Swaroop:** GITAM University, Visakhapatnam, India; E-mail: mjaswaroop@gmail.com

future. Over and over again, education is cited as a deciding factor when it comes to solving problems such as poverty, overpopulation, environmental degradation, and gender inequality. Education is the foundation of any country's economy. Many countries and institutions have remodelled their education system and implemented a new way of learning. Finland remains among the top nations in the Program for International Student Assessment (PISA) education survey. Finnish adults, according to international comparison, enjoy an admirable level of work-life balance. One open secret about the success of Finnish education is that regardless of geographical location or socioeconomic background, the same high standard education is available to children all over the country. At the Mind Valley, learning is a lifelong adventure. Isha Vidya preserves village identities and culture to enhance the boundaries of one's perception by educating rural India. In 1988, Wangchuk founded the student's educational and cultural moment of Ladakh (SECMOL) for reforming Ladakh's educational system by introducing life skills with the central government's pilot project for schools.

Holding students back in a classroom where they have failed to learn does not improve learning without changing anything about the teaching-learning process. Students remain unemployed after they complete their education. In most of the cases, teachers are poorly paid, which ultimately affects their interests. Thus, they are forced to opt for other alternatives such as tuitions in order to earn money. Besides this, teachers are also burdened with a non-academic workload which diverts their focus. Thus, the quality of the education drops, and students are forced to spend additional money to avail themselves tuition facilities. High dropout rates are also a serious challenge, especially in the case of girls. An absence of teachers during their duty timings is another problem. Management committees are hardly functional. Furthermore, parents are unaware of their rights and do not know whom to approach in such situations. Most of their funds which are allotted for the development, get consumed by intermediaries. True beneficiaries are only able to get a certain part of their fund. Education discriminates against people and will create differences from an early age in the name of competition. People blindly accept some facts that restrict their ideas in the process of learning. In some cases, education might fail to help students think big and smart. We are training students to waste 20 minutes of an hour, i.e., the first 10 minutes for a teacher to come to class and the last 10 minutes to take attendance. In a day, each student wastes more than 4 hours. In the long run, it will become a pattern and form habits that lead to addiction, unemployment eventually depression in adults. Moreover, in higher education institutions, the huge gap in acquiring practical knowledge and theoretical knowledge leads to unemployment, violent activities, and poverty. According to the Annual Status of Education Report (ASER) study in 2018, Students are lagging in reading skills. Education is more focused on results rather than on continuous learning. The challenges and solutions are presented in Table **1**.

CHALLENGES AND SOLUTIONS

Table 1. List of some challenges and possible solutions to Higher Education Institutes.

S.No.	Challenges	Solutions
1)	Infrastructure deficit	1. Building good infrastructure. 2. Adopting the latest technology.
2)	Quality of teachers	1. Training teachers. 2. Respecting teachers and giving them a salary that is higher than any other profession's. 3. Adopting the latest technology. 4. Encouraging teachers to only concentrate on their teaching work and improving students as human beings in society by keeping the psychological aspect in mind.
3)	High dropout rates	1. Building good infrastructure by reducing travel distance. 2. Adopting the latest technology. 3. Changing parents' mindsets.
4)	Restriction of personal thoughts	Informing parents and teachers to encourage natural ways of learning through play-based education.
5)	Adoption of technology	Encouraging parents and teachers to provide technology to children only after positively shaping their mindsets. Otherwise, students' minds might be manipulated by technology. Technology is addictive.
6)	Discrimination	Encouraging parents and teachers to positively shape children's mindsets. Students with good thinking and mindset will feel that all are equal.
7)	Teaching-learning process	Implementing concepts of story-based leaning, Play, and exploration, fast learning techniques.
8)	Time management	Conducting 5 to 10 minutes of activities that improve children's creativity. In the long run, these works will help them lead their life in society. Parents and teachers should take responsibility for assigning these small activities.

Learning Stages and Possible Approaches

It is well known that development of human beings is intricately connected to the growth and transformation of education (R. N. Sharma & R. K. Sharma, 2012). Fig. (**1**) suggests a new framework for reshaping the future of education that will give students the freedom to blossom and encourage them to study for recreation naturally.

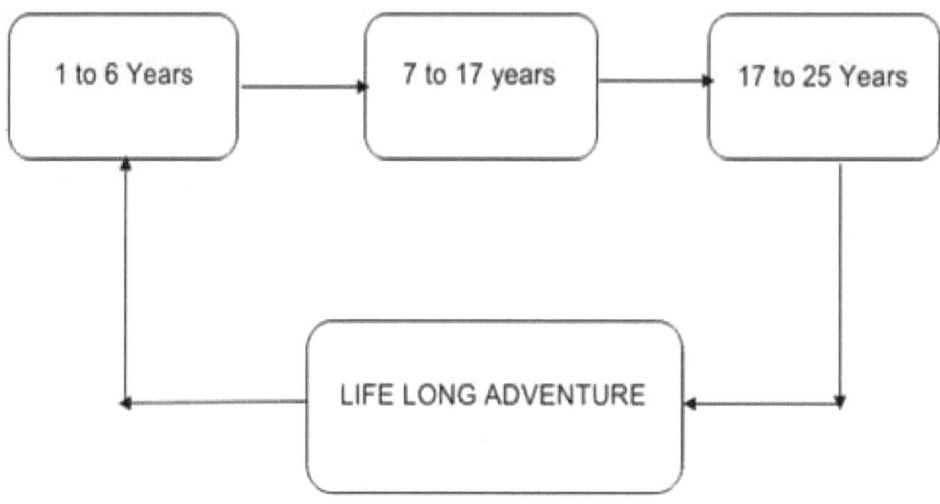

Fig. (1). Framework for reshaping the future of education.

Early Childhood Care and Education {1 to 6 Years}

We, parents and teachers, have the responsibility to create situations that will help each child in understanding the value of education from an early age. According to research, the real learning starts through inner programming at the age of 2 to 3. Children observe elder's thoughts and opinions and fill their subconscious minds with those beliefs. The information which you have today belongs to other people. Your talent is given to you when you're born. Your job is to reach deep down in yourself and discover it. According to the Wardha Scheme of Education 1937, education should be around some form of manual and productive work that is based on the environment of the child throughout the first seven years. Each child has innate abilities that must be discovered, nurtured, and developed through natural ways of learning, *i.e.,* by play-based education in groups and individually to build important lifelong skills.

Identify Natural Gifts and Passion {7 to 17 Years}

According to Khalil Gibran, "Your children are not your children. Parents should not impose their choices on children because they are sons and daughters of life's longing for itself." The passion you have in 7 to 17 is the gift that you have given to the world. Your hobbies may become your natural gifts and passion. Before completing 17 years, students should build their knowledge and identify their interests. After identifying their interest, they should go to a friend and talk about that area. If it gives them energy, if it excites them, then that is their passion. Inner programming decides your decision-making skills. If your sons/daughters have good inner programming, then they will make good decisions that lead to their passion, purpose, and mission. So, Inner programming plays a major role in being successful in our lives.

Passion Achieving {17 to 25 Years}

According to the Kothari Education Commission (1964–1966), the introduction of work experience and social service are integral parts of general education. Educational institutions should recognize their responsibility in facilitating the transition of youth from the world of school to the world of work and life. If you have a passion for something, then you have a strong interest in it, and you pursue it. If you identify your passion before the age of 17, it becomes an easy task to deal with it and attempt to overcome problems and difficulties in the future. Wealth and success are not connected to passion. The number one reason why most people don't get what they want is that they don't know what they want (T. Harv Eker, 2005).

According to psychological research, if you do things to relieve tension instead of achieving your dream, then you could go through a crisis at the age of 35. At the age of 35, you might think that you are not doing what you love to do. Hence, in my opinion, it is better to identify your interest and do your best work as early as possible. A lifelong learning experience enriches your thinking in a practical way. You end up loving the work that you do (Louise Hay, 2005).

Lifelong Adventure

If students have an interest in their work, then they will feel that learning is a lifelong adventure, and they will continuously update their knowledge, thinking, and mindset. Teachers should teach the process of learning to students, and they should make the students lifelong learners (Kiritkumar R. Chauhan, 2017). You are the only one who decides your decisions and habits. You are the only one who creates new decisions and new habits. This is the time to prove your existence in nature by making the world beautiful. We must rethink the purpose of education to prepare students for life and not just for exams. Knowledge expands our thoughts to a greater perspective which leads to inventions of unbelievable things. These inventions will be useful in making the world a better place. If you follow your passion and reach a higher position and create things from that position, you played your role in the country. Similarly, If everyone follows their passion and reaches their positions and creates things from their positions, then the world will become beautiful.

CONCLUSION

Learning is a continuous process for both the teacher and student. Learning is a combination of love and earning. We will become lifelong learners by doing what we love. Teachers are expected to concentrate on teaching and activities along with exploring new methods of improving students as human beings in society by considering their innate abilities, preferences, and psychological aspects. Students become good researchers if they are correctly trained in reading, writing, and learning the subjects keenly. In research-based learning, students make initial investigations in their topic, then conduct a study and finally evaluate their findings. This research-based learning will give a deeper understanding of the topics which students have chosen based on their interests. Then, this concept will remove words like failure and depression from the world. Eventually, this learning will create a new world of thinking. Institutes can apply educational learning stages that will help students to perform better in their lives by creating a good mindset. Public perception, which is a key factor in the ranking process, will improve in this process.

CONSENT FOR PUBLICATION

Not applicable.

CONFLICT OF INTEREST

The author declares no conflict of interest, financial or otherwise.

ACKNOWLEDGEMENTS

First, I am thankful to my parents, who supported and encouraged me in successfully completing my work. I would like to thank Vishen Lakhiani and T. Harv Eker, who guided me through their courses.

REFERENCES

Chauhan, Kiritkumar R. (2017). A Study of Thinking on Education System of Dr. A. P. J. Abdul Kalam. International. *Journal of Research in all Subjects in Multi Languages,* 5(8), 17-22. http://www.raijmr.com/ijrsml/wp-content/uploads/2017/11/IJRSML_2017_vol05_issue_08_Eng_04.pdf

Harv Eker, T (2005). Secrets of Millionaire Mind. Mastering inner game of wealth, 1st Edition, Harper Collins Business. USA, New York. https://www.amazon.in/Secrets-Millionaire-Mind-Mastering-Wealth-ebook/dp/B000FCJZ3G

Hay, Louise (2005). You can heal your life. UK, London: Hay House Inc. https://www.amazon.in/You-Can-Heal-Your-Life/dp/0937611018

Sharma, R.N., Sharma, R.K. (2012). History of Education in India. New Delhi: Atlantic Publishers and Distributors. https://www.amazon.in/History-Education-India-R-N-Sharma/dp/8171566006

CHAPTER 8

Importance of Professional Life Skills

K. Suryachandra Rao[1,*]

[1] *Principal Goverment Degree College Pathapatnam Srikakulam, India*

Abstract: In the present-day world, possessing a set of skills is the most important thing to get a suitable job. A set of basic rules that are acquired through everyday work experience is termed professional life skills. These skills enable people to deal with different issues, tasks and challenges effectively, which one faces daily. One needs them to survive in the world for livelihood. In short, any skill which is used to deal with problems in life can be considered a life skill. Life skills are not only essential but also important as these bring success and wealth in the life of an individual. In this 21st century, all these skills are essential to keep individuals ahead of others in this competitive world. Those skills are useful not only for a healthy society but also for successful individuals. Working in teams, communication, problem-solving, initiative and enterprise, planning and organization, self-awareness, positive attitude, and technology skill are also considered professional life skills. The skill of adaptability is crucial for survival and enables humans to transform themselves to fit into the environment. Problem-solving is a primary skill, which can contribute to one's professional success.

Keywords: Adaptability, Body language, Communication, Critical and lateral thinking, Emotional intelligence, Empathy, Flexibility, Information technology, Information transfer, Networking, Problem-solving skills.

INTRODUCTION

In a constantly changing environment, having life skills is a basic part of being able to address the difficulties of regular day to day existences. To be able to cope up with the increasing pace and change of present-day life, students need to hone certain skills, for example, the capacity to manage pressure and disappointment. They have to develop their skills and improve their employability opportunities. It is also the need of the hour to equip themselves with professional life skills. Much emphasis has been laid on smart work than on hard work in their respective fields. Ease of doing things has been appreciated than unnecessary drudgery.

---

* **Corresponding author K. Suryachandra Rao:** Principal Goverment Degree College Pathapatnam Srikakulam, India; Tel: 9849137382; E-mail: kscrao123@gmail.com

Sankara Narayana Rao Gedala and P.L. Saranya (Eds)
All rights reserved-© 2021 Bentham Science Publishers

BENEFITS FOR THE INDIVIDUALS

Skillful people across the globe are not only in great demand in the job market but also earn more. India needs more than 100 million skilled workers by 2022. In this regard, companies are not giving much importance to university degrees or certificates but looking for employability skills. They consider smartness, personality, and commitment in their selection process. Students with special skills are in high demand in the International Job market. The following are some of the skills the employers look for among prospective employees.

1. Critical thinking to solve problems 2. Ability to take responsibility 3. Good confidence levels 4. Decision making power 5. Self-awareness 6. Multi-Tasking.

Skill development is important in the overall development of a student's personality. These learning skills not only open new vistas but also replenish individuals with skills like networking and communication. They go a long way in aiding the holistic development of a person. During the job application and interview process, employers look for applicants with two skills set: hard skills and soft skills (Doyle *et al*., 2018).

Hard skills can be acquired through constant training, and they are easy to quantify. These hard skills are often mentioned in the candidate's application and on his curriculum vitae and are easy for the employer or recruiter to recognize and assess. Examples of hard skills include Proficiency in other languages, Any Bachelors degree from a University, Typing speed, Computer programming, Software development, Data entry, Advanced controlled Design systems, Accounting, Microsoft Power Point, Graphic design, Web development, Database administration, Artificial Intelligence, Cloud Computing, *etc*.

Soft skills, on the other hand, are subjective skills that are much harder to quantify. These are also known as "Social Skills" or "Interpersonal skills." Soft skills relate to the way one interacts with other people at work place in particular and in public in general. Examples of soft skills include Oral and Written Communication skills, Detail Oriented, Customer Service, Good Organization, Problem Solving, Self-starting/Self motivated, work independently, Project Management, Time management, Dependability, Work ethics, Teamwork/team-oriented *etc*.

While certain hard skills are necessary for any person, employers are looking increasingly for job applicants with particular soft skills. These skills vary from person to person. Even if a person lacks a particular skill required by the company, one can high light a particular soft skill that one knows would be valuable in the position For example, Group discussions, project presentations and conclaves.

Skill Development in Today's World

In the past, much emphasis was laid on the acquisition of knowledge in the teaching learning process. Knowledge was imparted to acquire academic grades rather than skills among students. This created a huge gap between academic Institutions and the Industry and there is a paradigm shift in the teaching methods thereby giving importance to the requirements of the industry. In India, UGC (University Grants Commission) has introduced several Skill Development courses in colleges to enhance employability skills among students. Skill development can take place in the class by giving different tasks and projects to students in the class. Student activities like role play, peer to peer interaction and experimental learning must be encouraged.

COMMUNICATION SKILLS

It is universally acknowledged truth that having the ability to communicate with others made human beings superior to other creatures on this planet. Even today this principle holds good. There is a great need to study the importance of communication in the present context.

Communication is the transfer of information between two or more than two persons. Communication as a skill is essential to convey views and ideas among human beings. Human communication is the process by which thoughts and feelings of one person are conveyed to others with the help of verbal and non-verbal symbols. This process involves sharing of information, convincing others and establishing human relationships. In spite of many technologically advanced tools used in communication, language remains the most important element in the process of communication. "The ability to express oneself is perhaps the most important of all the skills, a man can possess". With the interdisciplinary approach becoming important in the study of communication, experts from Psychology and Sociology believe that not only verbal skills, but attitudes, persuasive skills, logical thinking and behavioral changes also create an impact on communication. The ability to communicate effectively with superiors, colleagues, and staff is essential, no matter what industry one works in. Workers in the digital world must know how to convey and receive messages effectively in person as well as *via* phone, email, and social media.

Here are the top ten communication skills that will make one stand out in today's job market:

Listening

Listening is a receptive skill and being a good listener is one of the best ways to be a good communicator. No one likes communicating with someone who only cares about putting in her two cents, and does not take time to listen the other person. Instead, practice active *listening*.

Active listening means paying close attention to what the other person is saying, asking clarifying questions, and rephrasing what the person says to ensure understanding. Through active listening, one can better understand what the other person is trying to say, and can respond appropriately. As a matter of fact, listening needs lot of patience, alertness and intelligence. It is one of the most important skills that one should possess for a successful career. Through constant practice one can improve one's aural skill.

Nonverbal Communication

One's body language, eye contact, hand gestures, and tone all color the message one is trying to convey. A relaxed, open stance (arms open, legs relaxed), and a friendly tone will make you appear approachable, and will encourage others to speak freely with you. Eye contact is also important. One should look at the conversing partner in the eye to show that he/she is focused on the person and the conversation. In job interviews candidates' attitudes and performance levels will be tested through their body language. These play a vital role in the selection process.

Clarity and Precision

The message should be conveyed in a simple and direct manner whether the speaker is speaking to a person in phone, or *via* email. Suitable words should be used and one should not use remote and obsolete words in the communication. Unnecessary jargon will create confusion in the person at the other end. Usage of high flown language should not be encouraged.

Affable Personality

Through a friendly tone, a personal question, or simply a smile, will encourage one's coworkers to engage in open and honest communication. This is important in both face-to face and written communication. A quick "I hope you all had a good weekend" at the start of an email can personalize a message and make the recipient feel more appreciated. The affable nature will forge healthy relationship in the communication process. An amicable person always wins others hearts and gets the work done.

Confidence

It is important to be confident in all interactions with others. Confidence shows other coworkers that the person believes in what he is saying. Showing confidence can be as simple as making eye contact or using a firm but friendly tone. One should be careful to be assertive but not to sound arrogant or aggressive. Skill and confidence are requisite traits in prospective candidates. A diffident person cannot be successful in his endeavors and nobody likes him.

Empathy

Even when one disagrees with an employer, coworker, or employee, it is important to understand and respect their point of view. Using as simple as " I understand where you are coming from" demonstrates that the person has been listening to other colleagues and respect their opinions. One should also be sensible to others feelings while conversing with others.

Open –mindedness

A good communicator should enter any conversation with a flexible, open mind. One should try to understand the person's point of view, rather than simply trying to get the message. By having a genuine dialogue with the dissenters, one will be able to have more honest, productive interactions.

Respect

People will be more open to communicating with a person if he conveys respect for them and their ideas. Simple actions like using a person's name, making eye contact, and actively listening to a person speaks will make the person feel appreciated. On the Phone, one should avoid distractions and stay focused on the conversation.

Feedback

Being able to appropriately give and receive feedback is an important communication skill. Managers and supervisors should continuously look for ways to provide employees with constructive feedback, through emails, phone calls, or weekly status updates. Giving feedback involves giving praise as well. Something as simple as saying "good job" to an employee can greatly increase motivation.

Picking the Right Medium

An important communication skill is to simply know what form of communication to use. Some serious conversations are almost always best done in person. People will appreciate the thoughtful means of communication, and will be more likely to respond positively.

LIFE SKILLS

Problem Solving

Problem solving is the process of finding solution to complex issues. These skills help students to take day-to-day issues in a better manner. Problem –solving skills help people work more efficiently with peers, co-workers, customers and partners. Effective problem solving skills enable people to first analyses a problem and its causes, identify its severity and think of alternative solutions. A systematic approach can involve four basic steps:

Define the problem

Think of possible alternatives/options

Assess and select a suitable alternative.

Apply Solution

Emotional Intelligence

Emotions automatically bring about certain physiological changes like increased heart rate, faster breathing, heightened muscular alertness *etc.*, these changes provide a surge of energy that helps in acting instantly. Emotions play a very crucial role in human beings lives and life without emotions cannot be imagined. It would then just be series of events that goes through mechanically.

Emotions are reactions arising from the Autonomic Nervous System over which humans have little control. They are a survival tool during emergencies; the extra source of energy it generates helps in immediately dealing with a threatening situation. However, not harnessing these powers properly can be disastrous. Channeling in the right direction and in a productive manner can bring rich rewards to the person.

Emotional Intelligence (EM) is the capacity to use and channel emotions appropriately. It is the capacity to recognize our own feelings, manage them well, and also understand the feelings of others. Emotional Intelligence is also about managing interpersonal relationships well. In other words, it is the ability to train and use the emotional mind.

The current generation is more emotionally disturbed. This is due to lack of faith in oneself and the present system. This created vacuum in the minds of the people and made them restless. On an average, people are lonely, depressed, frustrated, aggressive, unruly, nervous, impulsive, and prone to worry. On the one hand there is an increase in the number of educated persons, better paying jobs, better facilities and great purchase power; ironically, there is also an increase in the rate of suicide, crime, substance abuse and divorce.

Improved emotional intelligence directly contributes to our mental and physical well being. Therefore, people with a high EQ (emotional quotient) are known to have a healthier and longer life. One can improve one's emotional Intelligence through constant practice. Emotional intelligence has a much stronger role to play in the success of a person. It is the new yardstick of success. It is being recognized that people have a thinking mind as well as a feeling mind.

According to the earliest researchers of Emotional Intelligence, "emotional intelligence involves the ability to understand one's own and others' feelings and emotions."(Mayer,J.D *et al*, 1997). Emotional Intelligence has four levels: Perceiving emotion, Understanding emotions, reasoning with emotion, regulating emotions.

Emotional Competence

Emotional competence that is dependent on EI is a learnt trait. People who do well in their career and life have developed this competence over the years. To be emotionally intelligent one should develop the following qualities:

Self-awareness

Emotional competence begins with knowing oneself and recognizing one's emotions. People know more about others than about themselves. That is because they spend more time focusing on and observing other's behavior compared to their own. Self awareness involves emotional awareness and accurate self assessment. In an emotional state it is difficult to think, and one may feel confused; at such times quietly to analyses one's feelings helps.

Emotional Regulation

Emotional regulation is about controlling and managing our emotions. "There is no fundamental skill more fundamental than resisting impulse" (Goleman *et al.*,

1995). A person with high emotional intelligence will certainly know how to regulate and channel his emotional responses.

Resilence

In real life situation, people come across many situations that make them angry, sad, depressed or anxious. Being resilient or strong makes us cope well and overcome them without being in a stressed emotional state for long. This helps individuals to move on in life smoothly, overcome hurdles, learn from each problem and be prepared to face further challenges. The present Covid-19 scenario has thrown new challenges to the world and companies across the globe have adopted new methods of work culture to overcome the evils of the pandemic. It has taught people of this generation new lessons to overcome the hurdles and cope with the present situation. This situation forced people to go online for day to day activities as the situation is grim and serious.

Trustworthiness and Conscientiousness

Being honest and maintaining personal integrity determines the character of a person, making them reliable; it provides emotional strength and self confidence. Trustworthiness at the personal level also means being competent, putting one's best efforts into doing a job. Trustworthiness and competence go hand in hand. People with this trait own up responsibility for their performance and are ready to accept their mistakes. They are proactive and discharge their duties to the utmost satisfaction of their employers. This skill makes one more organized and accountable; this helps people in keeping commitments. People with these skills are rated as superior and valued workers in all contexts.

Fortitude

A person with high emotional intelligence exhibits courage and accepts responsibility for their mistakes and is unwilling to face the consequences of their actions. Such persons will also not hesitate to take up challenges however difficult they are. They show exceptional fortitude and rise to the occasion.

Flexibility

People who are adaptable are open to new ideas and are flexible, ever ready to learn and adjust to various situations. They see new opportunities or avenues in changed situations and do not feel upset or annoyed by newer developments. They are able to revise their plan and are able to simultaneously handle different situations by prioritizing.

Innovation

Being flexible contributes to one's ability of generating new ideas, thinking out-of-the box being creative and accepting ideas from different sources. People who are innovative will try to think various ways of doing things and solving problems. They always look out for novel things to do, keeping their motivation levels high.

Drive to Achieve

Being always ready to learn, setting new goals and striving to improve performance are important traits of an emotionally intelligent person. Such persons remain committed to their goals, are determined and display a 'never say die' spirit. They welcome challenges and ready to take risks in to promote work. Such people show zest for life and make this world a better place.

Sensitivity

To be able to understand others' feeling and needs is an essential part of being human; this quality also forms an integral part of emotional intelligence. People with this skill are kind, selfless and are always ready to help others. They share their skills and mentor people to help to grow. They often put others' need before their own and altruistic in nature.

Social Competence

'No man is an island, entire of itself' (Donne *et al.*, 1923). Man is a social animal and inclined to lead a gregarious life. Various social groups are formed with different cultures in the process of Evolution. These Social groups are made up of people from different backgrounds, attitudes, and thinking styles. Gender difference too plays an important role. Being able to understand the differences yet not have a prejudice or bias towards other groups is social competence. People with this skill can get along with others and work in a team effectively, have a good communication skill and a sense of humor.

Although 'regular' intelligence is important to get success in life, emotional intelligence is key to relating well to others and achieving one's goal (mind tools pg.23).

Team Work

Team work refers to getting along with people and working together to achieve common goals. This skill is essential to develop interpersonal skills and leadership qualities in students. Teamwork is an activity undertaken by a group of individually talented people, working collaboratively to achieve a common goal. Whatever the nature and scale of the work, whether it is a large business organization or a small village cooperative, teamwork can be used to produce optimum results because the productivity ratio of several minds working on the same task is invariably greater than that of an individual.

Adaptability

Adaptability is a quality of being able to adjust with people or new conditions. Students should be able to adapt themselves in different situations. The skill of adaptability is crucial for survival. While some people are better at being able to adapt than others, it is a skill that can be learnt. Part of adapting is also finding creative solutions to problems. One may have to think 'out of the box', indulge in 'lateral thinking', approach the problem from a different direction, ask others to give their inputs and modify similar solutions to suit a particular problem. Adaptability skills are particularly important for leaders. This is because they frequently have to analyze the consequences of their decisions, and then change their thinking if the results are not favorable. They should not become entrenched in their own beliefs, to the extent of being blind to their mistakes.

Assertive Skills

Assertiveness is the ability to express one's opinions, feelings and views freely and without letting emotions, dictate the manner of expression and communication. The need to assert oneself usually arises when there is a conflict that needs to be resolved. There is a distinction between assertion and aggression. When asserting oneself, one does not give offence to or hurt the person one is in conflict with.

Stress Management

This refers to active management of stress by applying various techniques like meditation, relaxation and exercising. Stress management plays vital role in today's world. In the present day competitive world students have to face a lot of stress to get success in their career. They must know how to manage stress otherwise they will fail in their endeavors. Some relaxation techniques like meditation, yoga and pranayama will definitely help students to cope with the day to day problems. These will help students to face challenges in their future jobs successfully.

Positive Attitude

"A person's attitude can be inferred from the things a person does" (Morgan *et al*., 1978). A positive attitude is indicative of a person's optimistic outlook-his/her belief that they can overcome challenges and can achieve success by positive thinking. When a person responds constructively to stress, has the confidence to deal with problems and tries to find opportunities in every situation, he/she is said to have a positive attitude. "Developing and sustaining a positive attitude needs continuous effort" (Ghosh *et al*., 2013). A person has to identify the negative traits in his/her personality. Then he/she has to systematically and diligently work at replacing those with positive ones. This can be done by adopting positive thinking and practicing it until it becomes a habit.

Creativity

Creativity is use of imagination and ideas to create something new. It helps students to come up with newer ideas. This also enables a student to take initiative. Instead of drudgery and routine mechanical hard work, students should be trained to think with open mind on their own. They are encouraged to take up tasks on their own and find out solutions independently.

I.T SKILLS

I.T stands for Information Technology. Having a basic idea of computer and smart devices is an important skill in today's tech-enabled world. International Literacy Day 2018 focuses on the theme 'Literacy and Skills development'. The theme aims to create awareness on knowledge and competencies required for employment and livelihood. Skill development plays crucial role in the overall development of a student. Personal development, learning skills not only increases the opportunities but will also empower individual skills like networking and communication that go a long way in aiding the overall development of a person. The Government of India (GOI) has launched a program *Scheme for higher education youth for apprenticeship and skills* (SHREYAS) for students in Degree courses, primarily non-technical with a view to introduce employable skills into their learning. Their concept is merging skills into degree education. This paper focuses not only acquiring knowledge but also developing certain skills among students.

Information Transfer, or presenting verbal accounts of facts to pictures and changing graphical representations to writing, involves learning how to restate a given body of material in different ways. It is one of the important skills for students in study as well as professionals at their work place. Information transfer is used specifically in the contexts of narration, physical and process description, listing and classifying, comparison and contrast, showing a cause-and-effect relationship, and generalizing from numerical data. Transferring information from verbal to graphic form and *vice-versa* is thus a very useful skill that helps employees in particular fields. There are different kinds of graphic representations: maps and plans, tables, graphs, diagrams, Bar charts, flow charts, pie charts, tree diagrams and pictograms. These have different uses. Bar charts make comparisons, pie charts show how something is divided, and line graphs show variations in data.

CONCLUSION

Skills and Knowledge are the driving forces of economic growth and social development for any country. As India moves progressively towards becoming a 'knowledge economy' it becomes increasingly important that the country should focus on advancement of skills and these skills have to be relevant to the emerging economic environment .The present NEP(New Education Policy) 2020 has also given much importance to the acquisition of skills among students. Once the curriculum is adopted and implemented India will become Super Skill Power in the world in the near future. As the world is reeling under the pressure of Covid-19 pandemic, there is a great need to develop life skills to survive and to promote congenial work ambience for the job seekers .This will bring back the economy on wheels for progress.

CONSENT FOR PUBLICATION

Not applicable.

CONFLICT OF INTEREST

The author declares no conflict of interest, financial or otherwise.

ACKNOWLEDGEMENTS

Declared none.

REFERENCES

Clifford, M. (2017). A brief introduction to psychology. *McGraw. Hill Education.* https://www.amazon.in/Brief-Introduction-Psychology-Clifford-Morgan/dp/0070994552

Donne, J. (1923). Donne's Devotion. *Cambridge University Press.* https://archive.org/details/devotionsuponeme00donnuoft

Doyle, A. (2018). Hard skills *vs* soft skills. https://www.thebalancecareers.com/hard-skills-*vs*-soft- skills-2063780

Ghosh, M. (2013). Positivity: A way of life. *Orient Blackswan.* https://www.amazon.in/Positivity-Way-Life-Manika-Ghosh/dp/8125053468

Goleman, D. (2009). Emotional intelligence. *Bloomsbury Publisher.* https://www.bloomsbury.com/uk/emotional-intelligence-9781408806203/

Sluyter, J.D., Salovey, P. (1997). Emotional development and emotional intelligence. Basic Books, https://www.amazon.com/Emotional-Development-Intelligence-Educational-Implications/dp/0465095879

Sundaravalli, G.M. (2015). A.S. communication & soft skills. *Orient Black swan,* 1 https://www.amazon.com/ COMMUNICATION-SOFT-SKILLS-VOL-1/dp/8125060103

CHAPTER 9

Leveraging ICT for Excellence in Higher Education Institutions using Standards and Criteria of Accreditation and Ranking

Pradeep Kumar[1,*], **Balvinder Shukla**[2] and **Don Passey**[3]

[1] *Amity Institute of Information Technology, Amity University, Uttar Pradesh, India*
[2] *Professor of Entrepreneurship, Leadership & IT, Amity University, Uttar Pradesh, India*
[3] *Professor of Technology Enhanced Learning, Lancaster University, Lancaster, United Kingdom*

Abstract: Knowledge and its application by the workforce is a critical factor for sustainable and economic developments. In order to gain competitive advantages, it is important for an organization to rely on manpower that has relevant skills and competencies to deliver expected results within stipulated time-frames and available resources. Higher Education (HE) plays a vital role in developing such competencies and moving industry-ready talent into a human resource. Information and Communication Technology (ICT) is a key enabler for functional efforts in the context, including quality assurance and enhancement in higher education. ICT is being used for improving the quality of education all over the world due to its numerous advantages. Our study is focused on unearthing the vital role of ICT for achieving excellence in higher education institutions (HEIs) using standards/criteria of various accreditation and ranking bodies. A survey was conducted using a Likert scale-based questionnaire including an open-ended question related to usage and importance of ICT for improving the quality of higher education. The results show that leveraging ICT can help higher education institutions (HEIs) to enhance overall quality through benchmarking institutional data, implementation and monitoring of best practices in pursuit of excellence.

Keywords: Academic activities, Accreditation, Alumni, DVV, Excellence, Government bodies, Higher Education, ICT, Inflibnet, Linkages, NAAC, Quality, Ranking, Satisfaction survey.

INTRODUCTION

Information and Communication Technology (ICT) is an extended term of Information Technology (IT) focusing additionally on the role of unified comm-

---

[*] **Corresponding author Pradeep Kumar:** Amity Institute of Information Technology, Amity University, Uttar Pradesh, India; E-mail: pkumar17@amity.edu

Sankara Narayana Rao Gedala and P.L. Saranya (Eds)
All rights reserved-© 2021 Bentham Science Publishers

unication technologies. ICT refers to the integration of telecommunications, computers, middle-ware and data systems that support, store and transmit unified communications between systems (Murray, James, 2011). ICT has a major role in fields regardless of the type of business, job, or service including quality assurance in higher education (Omollo, 2013, Haris, 2017) conducted a study on the utilization of ICT in quality assurance and accreditation of higher education. The study reveals that extensive usage of ICT in higher education has a positive impact on the processes, services and quality of education. Usage of ICT makes substantial changes in teaching-learning through enhanced distribution and ease of access to information. The use of ICT improves the learning environment and prepares learners for their future lives and careers (Habib, 2017). Passey *et al.* analyzed the importance of ICT in planning and implementing access and leveraging digital technologies for HEI in developing countries. They found that careful deployment of ICT helps HEIs to overcome issues related to data consistency, information flow, decision-making, and formation of policies. Each year, HEIs are generating data in large volumes, also in heterogeneous formats. Data analysis, creation of management information system (MIS) reports, availability of such reports anytime anywhere is beneficial in decision-making for the development of strategies, policies, academic and non-academic activities/processes and in continuous improvement (Hussain 2016).

For a large period of time, HEIs have had a vital role in national building through developing skilled manpower and developing changes in society which ultimately leads to societal transformation. Schindler *et al.* found that stakeholders have different opinions about quality and excellence in this respect, *e.g.* students associate quality of HEI through curriculum, teaching-learning facilities and student success, whereas faculty members link excellence with academic freedom, remuneration and funds, continuous growth, *etc.* Primarily, the level of stakeholders' satisfaction and students' success along with curriculum, infrastructure, research outcomes, support services and institutional governance determine the quality and excellence of higher education (Nandi and Chattopadhyay 2012). Kumar *et al.* emphasized on many excellence models in higher education including EFQM Excellence Model, Baldrige Model, Kanji's Model for Higher Education, Curtin Planning and Quality Framework, Garg's Operational Excellence Model. However, Excellence in H.E. is perceived and understood across the world as outstanding results of students' learning through a quality education, which may be benchmarked globally. According to Harvey and Green, 1993, there are three perceptions for excellence: A Conventional Concept: the conventional concept is related to the perception of uniqueness, or something distinct or 'elevated'. Surpassing High Standards: quite often excellence is perceived as high quality of standards. Evaluating Standards: A 'quality' service/product is one that has gone through an evaluation process and meets/complies with predefined standards/criteria which are based on achievable performance indicators.

The standards approach to quality implies that quality can be further improved if standards are raised. Excellence is also defined in a relative term, with reference to something that is inferior. It is defined as 'exclusivity', reinforces merit and positions an institution in some ranking (Little and Locke, 2011). In other words, we may say that excellence in higher education may be defined as meeting predefined standards/criteria with an outstanding position that can be demonstrated through an achieved status of grade/rank.

ACCREDITATION AND RANKING

Accreditation is a process to assure quality of an institution or program, which undergoes an external and independent review process by experts to assess if it meets the prescribed standards. Accreditation is used to understand the "Quality Status" of an institution (Lee, 2004, CHEA, 2010). NBA, 2019 highlights the purpose of accreditation as an instrument to promote and recognize excellence in higher education at program level. Hazelkorn, 2011 accentuated rankings as a manifestation of what has become known as the worldwide 'battle for excellence', and these are perceived and used to determine the status of individual institutions, assess the quality and performance of the higher education system and gauge global competitiveness.

Accreditation status assures the stakeholders that the HEI/program complies with standards defined by regulatory authorities and expert groups, whereas, ranking provides the status of institutional performance within a competitive set up (Nandi and Chattopadhyay, 2012). The classification of HEIs shows their strengths and provides the public with what are regarded as helpful, relevant data to inform high education decision making (Abdulla Al Karam, KHDA, 2019).

Various standards/criteria of evaluation have been defined by different accrediting and ranking bodies. Mapping of the standards/criteria of a few accrediting bodies, NAAC, WASC, and NBA, and ranking bodies, QS and THE, depicted in Table **1**, which reflects the following: 1) Criteria/standards of accrediting bodies revolve around the basic functioning of HEIs, such as curriculum, teaching-learning, research, infrastructure and learning resources, support facilities, governance, institutional values, and continuous improvements through quality assurance processes. However, parameters for rankings revolve around reputation survey/peer perceptions, availability of teaching-learning resources, faculty-student ratio, diversity of students & faculty and research outcomes (*i.e.* research & professional practices, citation per faculty, research income and international outlook/collaborations). 2) Another common factor is that every accrediting and ranking body requires the availability of relevant data/information in the public domain for general disclosure. 3) The study shows that weighting given for various criteria/standards by the respective accrediting/ranking bodies is different, shown in Table **1**. However, WASC, QAA and IET do not have a system of marks allocation for each independent criterion.

Table 1. Weighting allocated to research activities by accrediting and ranking bodies.

Accrediting Body		Ranking Body	
NAAC	25%	NIRF	20%
		QS	20%
		THE	65%

NBA has assigned weighting of 75 marks out of 1000 marks to research and development, *i.e.* 7.5%. In research, copyrights and patents also play important role, according to Sejersen and Hansen, 2018, augmented emphasis on patents is a key component to an international science policy revealed in particular through OECD statistics, where patenting serves as a key metric in international rankings. Innovation and patenting give recognition to the scholarly work of scholars' productivity, as measured by academic publications and citations, which interprets into scholars' professional achievement. The scholars' academic productivity increases university reputation and market value (Faria *et al*, 2018). Teaching learning weighting is shown in Table **2**.

Table 2. weighting given to teaching-learning and evaluation.

Accrediting Body		Ranking Body	
NBA	55.5%	NIRF	70%
NAAC	20%	QS	30%
		THE	35%

A reputation survey/feedback system is one of the common parameters. The QS Ranking System is highly focused on reputation survey, which has 50% weighting, *i.e.* Academic Reputation Survey, 40% weighting, and Employer Reputation Survey, 10%, whereas other ranking and accrediting bodies have 5% - 10% weighting for this parameter. Accreditation focuses on inputs, process and outputs whereas ranking emphasizes outputs/results. From the perspective of institutions, accreditation and ranking both help to identify gaps in a curriculum, delivery mechanism, academic and non-academic processes, various support services and finally output and outcomes. Accreditation and ranking both require data in high volumes, as data over a defined period, 3 – 5 years, is used for institutional/program evaluation. The process of accreditation and ranking requires a great deal of documentation and evidence-based evaluation which is labor intensive and error prone. ICT tools make this process of data handling and report generation more efficient and effective (Hussain, 2016).

The processes of accreditation and rankings have a few similarities and somewhat vary, which is shown in Table 2, which reveals the following:

Before Applying

Before applying for an accreditation, it is important to go through eligibility criteria and feasibility issues (related to operational and economic feasibility) whereas such requirements are not applied in ranking.

Submission of Initial Application

It is common in all accreditation and rankings to submit the application along with requisite supporting documents.

Submission of a Detailed Report

In every accreditation process, a detailed report, SSR/SAR/SED, *etc.*, is to be submitted upon acceptance of initial application, whereas in rankings, it is not applicable.

Data Validation and Verification (DVV) Process

Applicable to all accreditation and rankings. During this process, often additional documents or evidence in support of earlier submitted data are also required.

Satisfaction Survey

All accreditation and ranking bodies conduct a satisfaction/reputation survey. However, the difference comes in the categories of stakeholders. Accrediting bodies conduct and analyze a satisfaction survey from all stakeholders. Everything revolves around students. However, in rankings a reputation survey is conducted through faculty and employers only.

Site Visit

Most accrediting bodies conduct a site-visit to the HEI for a physical verification of facilities and processes. However, in rankings, a site-visit is not conducted. A ranking process involves only the data submission and verification through support documents and data availability on the web, institutional website and third party web site, *e.g.* Scopus, Web of Science, Inflibnet *etc.*

Declaration of Result

Once the above processes are successfully completed, the result is declared by the respective accrediting/ranking bodies in a stipulated timeframe.

Public Disclosure of Information

The results and relevant documents are published on the institutional website for public disclosure so that relevant stakeholders may access the useful information.

Submission of Annual Report and Annual Dues

Most accrediting bodies require the submission of an annual report, such as NAAC, WASC, IACBE, IET, *etc.*, while in ranking this process is not application because ranking is done each year whereas in accreditation there is a period of validity. The process of accreditation and ranking is further illustrated through a flow chart in Figs. (**1** and **2**), respectively.

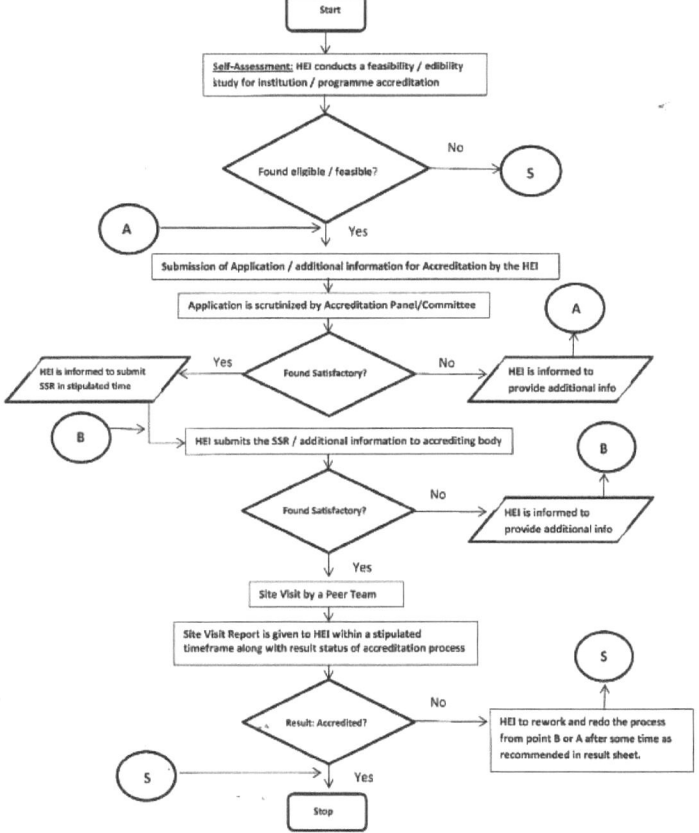

Fig. (1). Ranking process.

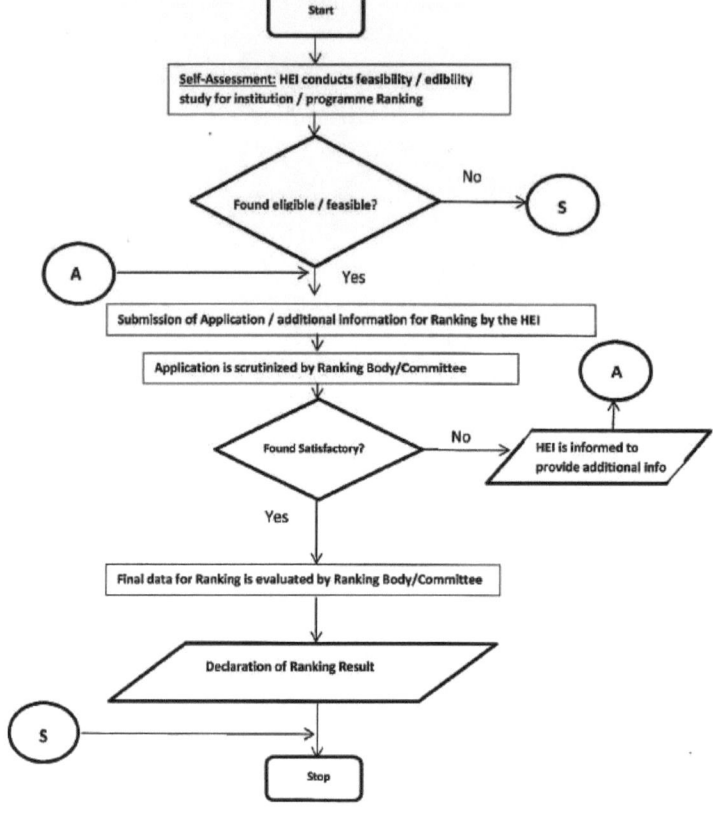

Fig. (2). Ranking process.

In the next section, we review the literature and present how ICT can be integrated in higher education for administering, monitoring and supporting quality improvements of institutional activities.

Role of ICT in Higher Education

Usage of the latest technologies in HEIs helps in better planning, implementation, monitoring/review, decision-making and taking preventive and corrective actions for quality improvements (Garg, 2015). Online education is gaining continuous momentum; and a common phenomenon in HEIs is to replace traditional blackboards with digital smart boards. Further, the importance of online and distance learning (ODL) has also been marked in the new education policy of India (Draft National Education Policy, 2019 chapter #10) that all HEIs may offer ODL programs based on the grade achieved in NAAC accreditation in order to enhance their offerings, improve access, rise gross enrollment ratio, and provide more prospects for lifelong learning. ICT is fundamental in ODL education. As well as supporting more regular learners, ICT enables various services/offerings such as creating alumni groups, community, sharing different searches in twitter, Linkedin and Facebook, *etc.*, enable students to find out about the reputation and education system of their institution. In this respect, academic and non-academic processes of HEIs are linked with administrative activities to monitor, review and make continuous improvements in education systems.

Ben-Zion Barta *et al.*, 1995 emphasized the usage of computers/IT for effective educational administration, for: Administration of Students' Data, Personal Record Maintenance, Payroll and Financial Accounting, General Administration, Learning Resource System, Inventory Management. Appropriately deployed ICT can support organizations in achieving their competitive advantages, market position, quality care of their stakeholders, and efficient operations. Also, ICT helps to reduce optional costs and increase revenues (Pamela Matthews, 2000). Garg *et al.*, 2015 explored the usage of ICT as a tool for operational excellence in the higher education sector. The study was conducted across following nine major functional departments of the HEIs: Admissions, Finance, Academics, Examinations, Human Resource, Industry Interaction and Placement Cell, Administration, Library, Hostel.

The research results of Garg and Shukla's study revealed that operational excellence of an HEI is achieved by aligning operations with targets and maintaining lower execution cost, high speed, optimum utilization of resources, improved flow of end-to-end information, improvement in manpower efficiency, MIS generation, and availability of relevant information as and when requirement at any place. In this ways, ICT plays a vital role to manage day-to-day operations and to achieve operational excellence.

The Draft National Education Policy of India, 2019, chapter #19 highlights the leveraging that technology can bring in H.E. categorized into the following 4 broad groups: Preparation of Teaching Staff: A train-the-trainer program is very important. Teaching staff must acquire relevant training in how to use the appropriate technology to enhance students' learning outcomes. Teaching Learning and Evaluation: Modern tools based on technology can be applied in teaching-learning and evaluation. Reach to Education: Education must be within reach for all socioeconomic groups of societies, including specially-able students and diverse groups of remote areas. Governance: Strategic planning for long/short term, academic and non-academic administration and day-today-management of an HEI need to be ICT enabled. The integration of ICT in higher education is depicted in Fig. (**3**).

Fig. (3). Integration of ICT in higher education.

Leveraging ICT in Accreditation and Rankings of Higher Education Institutions

The ICT is closely integrated in today's higher education system. In this section, the role of ICT in each and every criterion and processes of accreditation and rankings of HEIs is summarized. Table **3** shows a summary of ICT roles related to the various study elements/criteria of accreditation and rankings. These study elements are drawn by analyzing the criteria of various accrediting and ranking bodies, such as NAAC, IET, AACSB, NIRF, THE.

Table 3. Summary of ICT roles.

S. No.	Study Element/Accreditation & Ranking Criteria	Role of ICT – A glance
1	Curricular Aspects	• ICT tools for gathering opinions/inputs of various stakeholders for curriculum development and review. • ICT tools for e-content development • Linkage with current industrial and technological updates • ICT tools in completion of projects and other study assignments in faster and reliable ways.

(Table 3) cont.....

S. No.	Study Element/Accreditation & Ranking Criteria	Role of ICT – A glance
2	Teaching-Learning and Evaluation	• Easy student enrollment process • Students can make their own basket of courses based on their interest and disciple of study through ICT-enabled 'choice based credit systems' • Flexibility to develop students' time-table of various study sessions • Enables student to learn round the clock • Online monitoring of academic sessions • Mapping of intended educational objectives (PEOs) with learning outcomes (SLOs) is much easier and faster through ICT • ICT-enabled grievance readdress systems help to collect, analyze and to take appropriate action in time • ICT helps in faster and reliable evaluation of faculty/staff using online tools for performance appraisal systems • Online examination system provides transparency and better control of examination related activities and evaluation of results • Display of results within stipulated timeframe • Calculation of pass percentage (programme-wise, course-wise and faculty-wise) can be done and accordingly necessary planning/action can be taken in shortest times.
3	Research, Innovation and Extension	• ICT helps in data gathering and analysis • Enhancing collaborative research initiatives through reliable technological links and tools • Powerful computing systems that interpret complex research situations • Speedy production/publication of research materials • Research publications are safe from malpractices checking through plagiarism and other online tools • Relevant policies, guidelines for research can be easily accessed by students, researchers, scholars and faculty/staff • Reusable formats are developed • HEIs may apply for various national/international research grants and awards using ICT • Technology transfer and implementation of research outcomes • Availability of research publications anywhere anytime • Translation of results in multiple languages. • Helps to conduct webinars and professional development programmes for skill enhancement, *etc.*
4	Infrastructure and Learning Resources	• ICT-enabled facilities (such as smart classes, learning management system (LMS), Wi-Fi/LAN) and infrastructure for reported better learning experiences • Time independent and remote access of learning resources • Portable and mega content storage • Availability of a single material at many places concurrently • Easy content posting and modification.

(Table 3) cont.....

S. No.	Study Element/Accreditation & Ranking Criteria	Role of ICT – A glance

5	Student Support and Progression	• ICT offers faster facilities to students of other states and nationalities
		• ICT helps in student capacity enhancement and development through various tools such as language laboratories, guidance for competitive examinations, online (and personal level also) counseling and guidance
		• ICT plays an important role in students' progression:
		   o For Higher Education: Interacting with various other HEIs regardless of geographical boundaries
		   o For Entrepreneurship and Start-ups: Understanding and linkages with supply-chain and competitive organizations
		   o For Placement: Skill development and interaction with multiple organizations in short time. Online interviews and career opportunities
		• Students get instant information about various schemes (scholarships/freeships), activities (curricular and extra-curricular), events and supporting their participation accordingly
		• Alumni engagement.

6	Governance, Leadership and Management	• Improves control over policy formulation by analyzing a wide data spectrum
		• Provides information to facilitate decision-making at management level for seeking improvements across all levels
		• ICT tools provide for better projections, forecasting and strategic planning
		• Better decentralization and participative management beyond physical locations and time restrictions
		• Implementation of e-governance:
		   o Planning and development
		   o Administration
		   o Finance and accounts
		   o Student admissions and support
		• Quality assurance through automatic checks/alarming systems over absentees, course progress, research outcomes, examination results, placements, *etc.* (besides in-person inspections and monitoring).
		• Tracking the incremental improvement of HEI over a period of time.

Each accreditation and ranking process require supporting documents of every activity related to the above study elements/criteria shown in Table **3** for multiple years. Online managed record keeping helps HEIs with easy storage, analysis, generation of MIS reports in different formats as prescribed by various accreditation and ranking bodies and makes them available for further processing/usage. As it is evident that the processes of higher education are covered through accreditation and ranking, an automated accreditation and certification system was developed and patented in US Patent Application Publication by in February 2005 to streamline the processes, minimizing the period of the on-site survey, eliminating paper-work and transfer of documents electronically. In next section, the authors elaborate the research methods of analysis, findings and concluding observations concerning implications of the research study.

Methodology

Goddard and Melville, 2004 explained methodology as answering unanswered questions or exploring a situation which currently does not exist in a research literature. The objective of this section is to explain the tools and techniques used for data collection, analysis and interpretation of data related to usage of ICT in HEIs. The present study was conducted in the HEIs of National Capital Region (Delhi/NCR). **Sample size:** 452 faculty and staff members. **Tool(s) for data collection:** Respondents were asked to participate in a survey based on the research questionnaire on the usefulness of ICT for enhancing the excellence of HEIs in reference to enabling accreditation and ranking processes. The ten parameters shown in Table 4 following were used in the questionnaire, using a 5-point Likert scale, where 1 means 'strongly disagree and 5 means 'strong agree':

Table 4. Parameters used in the Research Questionnaire.

Parameters
MIS and report generation
Improve flow of information across institutions/departments
Consistency of data
Save time
Reduce wastage of resources
Cost reduction
Access of information anywhere anytime
Convenience of work
Increase efficiency in day-to-day management activities
Less human intervention - save manpower

Data Analysis: MS-Excel and SPSS were used for analysis of data.

Statistical Techniques used for Data Analysis

To bring the data into a simple comparable form in Microsoft (MS) Excel, the percentage of responses in the different categories (strongly agree to strongly disagree) has been calculated, where 'strongly agree' and 'agree' are calculated as 'agree', and 'strongly disagree' and 'disagree' are calculated as 'disagree'. To gain statistical results using SPSS, a t-test has been applied in the present study.

Findings and Discussions

ICT is useful in data compilation, analysis, communication, interaction, collaboration and in accessing the information beyond geographical boundaries. Leveraging ICT may also help in improvement of teaching-learning and overcoming issues and challenges in education sectors (Garg and Shukla, 2017). When ICT is applied in an HEI to the criteria/standards of accreditation and rankings, according to responses, better results can be obtained in every criteria and process. Fig. (**4**) shows the mean score of parameters. High mean score shows the level of importance of leveraging ICT in respective areas.

Fig. (4). Mean Score of parameters.

Today, worldwide e-contents are being developed. MOOCs and other online courses are being developed and emphasized that they can cover and support a mass generation worldwide, in that they are very competitive in terms of cost and user convenience time-frames. Students can study anywhere anytime; project/field based studies are offering preferences; curriculum are being updated with the latest technological trends; courses are offered with multiple choices. The importance of ICT in these respects is clearly illustrated from results shown in Fig. (**5**).

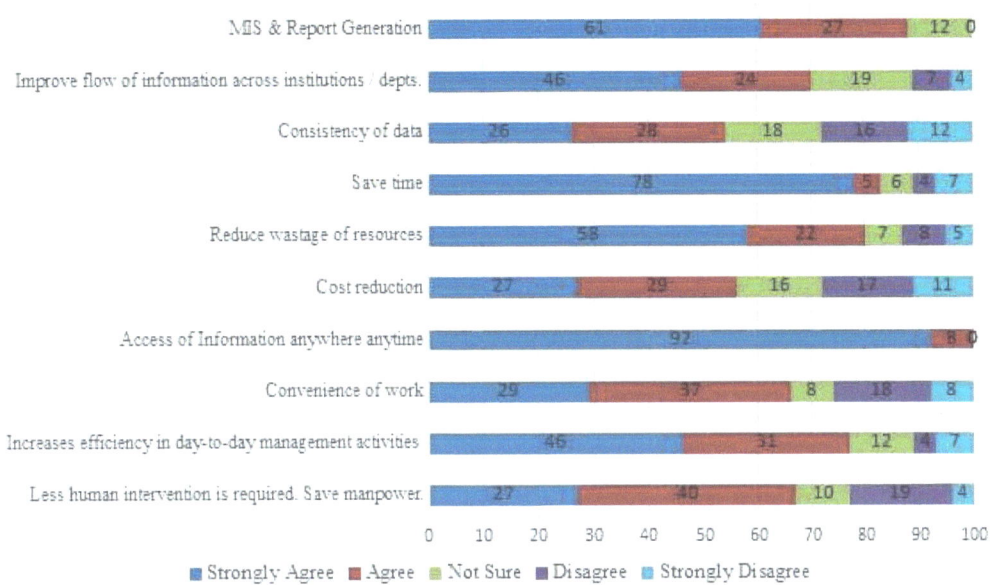

Fig. (5). Importance of ICT (Data presented in percentage).

Fig. **(5)** shows that the majority, 88% of the respondents agreed that ICT plays an important role in management information system (MIS) and the generation of relevant reports and only 12% of the respondents were not sure. The flow of information across institutions/departments is clearly very important in that there is a need for all key personnel to receive similar data in order to take appropriate decisions. 70% of respondents agreed on this. Data consistency is shown to be very important for all processes; without consistency, data may have redundancies. 54% respondents agreed, 18% were not sure and 28% disagreed as they still were happy to use the old system of paper records. All respondents agreed, *i.e.* 100%, that ICT extends support to access information anywhere anytime and 83% agreed that it saves time. Ten percent of respondents were not sure that usage of ICT saves manpower, while 23% of respondents thought that still the same amount of human effort is required even if ICT is used. The survey results were statistically tested using one-sample t-tests on SPSS, as illustrated in Table **5**.

The mean value for the parameters is 2.5, which is statistically significantly different from the test value of 3. We may conclude that the results shown in Table **5** have a significantly higher mean on the parameters than 3. The t value of the parameter "Access of information anywhere anytime" is 150.630, which is the highest amongst all parameters. In other parameters, the 2-tailed significance value indicates the usefulness of ICT for achieving excellence in HEIs in reference to enabling accreditation and ranking processes. However, the study shows that still many staff members may need personal development training on the usage of ICT and to learn how using ICT can be comfortable in their work and save human intervention by automation of processes.

Table 5. t-test result.

	t	df	Sig. (2-tailed)	Mean Difference	95% Confidence Interval of the Difference	
					Lower	Upper
Less human intervention is required. Save manpower.	12.117	451	.000	.670	.56	.78
Increases efficiency in day-to-day management activities	19.001	451	.000	1.049	.94	1.16
Convenience of work	9.968	451	.000	.606	.49	.73
Access of information anywhere anytime	150.630	451	.000	1.920	1.90	1.95
Cost reduction	7.004	451	.000	.440	.32	.56
Reduce wastage of resources	21.573	451	.000	1.197	1.09	1.31
Save time	25.144	451	.000	1.427	1.32	1.54
Consistency of data	6.411	451	.000	.405	.28	.53
Improve flow of information across institutions/depts.	18.759	451	.000	1.007	.90	1.11
MIS and Report Generation	45.292	451	.000	1.491	1.43	1.56

CONCLUSION

The numbers of HEIs are increasing rapidly, due to huge increases in the global population and demands of accessing quality education. Aspirants/students are traveling to global destinations to acquire what they consider to be the best education. Many parents and students are taking educational loans to seek the best career through a globally-recognized degree. In many countries, students' debts are also increasing year on year. In such a scenario, the biggest question that arises is how to ensure that an institution offers the best education, since every HEI claims that they are the best. Accreditation and ranking are tools that seek to ensure the quality of curriculum, faculty, research, infrastructure and learning resource, learning outcomes and students' success rates. Accreditation is the process to ensure that an HEI is complying at least with the minimum requirements, while the outcomes/results of applied processes, policy guidelines and various strategic plans are measured through rankings. Research and Patents which are highly emphasized both in accreditation and rankings exhibit the amount of intellectual work and academic reputation of an institution. It is no exaggeration in saying that accreditation and rankings are perceived as quality stamps in higher education that defines level of excellence.

Availability of reliable, consistent, and authentic data is a primary requirement for accreditation and rankings and ICT plays a vital role in this area. Using ICT, symmetry can easily be maintained in the data. For example, a student's data entered by the admissions department can be utilized by teaching faculty, non-teaching staff, the examination department, a student's support department, and so on, without repeating the same entries again and again. In each accreditation and ranking, data of the last 3–5 years is required. Keeping such data in huge volumes without redundancy and in a form to compute for further analysis and to present in various formats as prescribed by different accrediting and ranking bodies is difficult if this is done without applying appropriate ICT. Therefore, leveraging ICT in data management as per requirements, *i.e.* criteria/standards of various accrediting and ranking bodies, leads an HEI towards achieving excellence in higher education. Many accrediting and ranking bodies have already developed frameworks for their respective accreditation and rankings, *e.g.* NAAC, NBA, AACSB, NIRF, QS, THE. Yet, no common framework exists so far which has an integrated approach of functioning, with processes of criteria/standards using ICT enabled functioning. In the future, the results of this study may be utilized and developed to design an ICT enabled model framework for excellence in HEIs, with special reference to accreditation and ranking.

CONSENT FOR PUBLICATION

Not applicable.

CONFLICT OF INTEREST

The author declares no conflict of interest, financial or otherwise.

ACKNOWLEDGEMENTS

Declared none.

REFERENCES

Abdulla Al Karam, (KHDA, 2019). https://thepienews.com/news/uk-dominates-in-dubais-inaugural-branch-campus-ratings/

Academic Ranking of World Universities. (2019). http://www.shanghairanking.com/ ARWU-Methodology-2018.html

Accreditation, A.A.C.S.B. (2019). https://www.aacsb.edu/accreditation/journey/ process-overview

Accreditation, W.S.C.U.C. (2019). https://www.wscuc.org/resources/eligibility

Anchal, G., Balvinder, S., Graham, K. (2015). Information technology as a tool for operational excellence in the education sector. http://shodhganga.inflibnet.ac.in/bitstream/10603/188965/10/cover%20page.pdf

CHEA (2010), The value of accreditation. https://www.acpe-accredit.org/pdf/ValueofAccreditation.pdf

Draft National Education Policy of India. (2019). https://mhrd.gov.in/sites/upload_files/mhrd/files/Draft_NEP_2019_EN_Revised.pdf

Emon, N., Saumen, C. (2012). Quality, accreditation and global university ranking: issues before Indian higher education. *India Infrastructure Report 2012*. https://www.taylorfrancis.com/books/e/9781134952588/chapters/10.4324/9781315538914-27

Faria, J.R., Wanke, P.F., Ferreira, J.J., Mixon, F.G., Jr (2018). Research and innovation in higher education: empirical evidence from research and patenting in Brazil. *Scientometrics, 116*(1), 487-504.
[http://dx.doi.org/10.1007/s11192-018-2744-4]

Garg, A., Shukla, B. (2017). IT implementation in the education sector: a review, 2017 international conference of electronics, communication and aerospace technology (ICECA).
[http://dx.doi.org/10.1109/ICECA.2017.8212737]

Goddard, W., Melville, S. (2004). *Research Methodology: An Introduction..* Lansdowne: Juta and Company Ltd. https://www.amazon.in/Research-methodology-introduction-Social-Statistics/dp/0702156604

Habib, Hadiya (2017). Role of ICT in higher education. *International Journal of Creative Research Throughts (IJCRT), 5*(4). https://ijcrt.org/papers/IJCRT1704371.pdf

Harvey, L. (2004). The power of accreditation: views of academics. *J. High. Educ. Policy Manage., 26*(2), 207-223.
[http://dx.doi.org/10.1080/1360080042000218267]

Harvey, L., Green, D. (1993). Defining quality. *Assess. Eval. High. Educ., 18*.
[http://dx.doi.org/10.1080/0260293930180102]

Hazelkorn, E. (2015). *Globalization and the Reputation Race. In: Rankings and the Reshaping of Higher Education..* Palgrave Macmillan.London:
[http://dx.doi.org/10.1057/9781137446671_1]

Hussain, M., Al-Mourad, M.B., Mathew, S.S. (2016). Collect, Scope, and Verify Big Data – A Framework for Institution Accreditation.
[http://dx.doi.org/10.1109/WAINA.2016.45]

Jiao, X. (2005). Automated accreditation system. https://patentimages.storage.googleapis.com/18/ad/59/6c3416db867105/US20050028005A1.pdf

Little, B., Locke, W. (2011). Conceptions of excellence in teaching and learning and implications for future policy and practice. In: Rostan, M., Vaira, M., (Eds.), *Questioning Excellence in Higher Education. Higher Education Research in the 21st Century Series* Sense Publishers.
[http://dx.doi.org/10.1007/978-94-6091-642-7_7]

Matthews, P. (2000). Leveraging technology for success. *J. Healthc. Inf. Manag., 14*(2), 5-12. https://s3.amazonaws.com/rdcms-himss/files/production/public/HIMSSorg/Content/files/jhim/14-2/him14202.pdf
[PMID: 11066648]

Murray, James (2011-12-18). "Cloud network architecture and ICT - Modern Network Architecture". TechTarget =ITKnowledgeExchange.

NAAC Accreditation (2019). http://naac.gov.in/index.php/assessment-accreditation#accreditation

NBA Accreditation (2019). http://www.nbaind.org/accreditation.aspx#accreditation-process

Passey, D., Laferrière, T., Ahmad, M.Y-A., Bhowmik, M., Gross, D., Price, J., Resta, P., Shonfeld, M.

(2016). Educational digital technologies in developing countries challenge third party providers. *J. Educ. Technol. Soc., 19*(3), 121-133. http://www.research.lancs.ac.uk/portal/en/publications/educational-digital-technologies-in-developing-countries-challenge-third-party-providers(06ee06da-a1dd-4de7-b89c-47c4a64de540)/export.html

https://www.qs.com/rankings-process-in-brief/ QS Ranking (2019)

R., Omollo, J., Ondulo, P., Kemei (2013). The role of ICT in appreciating tri-axis efforts of research, publications and library services in higher education. *2013 IST-Africa Conference & Exhibition,* 1-9. https://ieeexplore.ieee.org/stamp/ stamp.jsp?tp=&arnumber=6701753&tag=1

Sajjad, H.A., Hironori, W., Yoshiaki, F. (2017). Utilization of ICTs in Quality Assurance and Accreditation of Higher Education: Systematic Literature Review. *2017 IEEE International Conference on Teaching, Assessment, and Learning for Engineering (TALE),* 354-359. [http://dx.doi.org/10.1109/TALE.2017.8252361]

Schindler, L., Puls-Elvidge, S., Welzant, H., Crawford, L. (2015). Definitions of quality in higher education: A synthesis of the literature. *Higher Learning Research Communications, 5*(3), 3-13. [http://dx.doi.org/10.18870/hlrc.v5i3.244]

Sejersen, N., Hansen, J. (2018). From a Means to an End: Patenting in the 1999 Danish 'Act on Inventions' and its Effect on Research Practice. *Minerva, 56*(3), 261-281. [http://dx.doi.org/10.1007/s11024-017-9336-y]

Times Higher Education Ranking. (2019). https://www.timeshighereducation.com/world-university-rankings/methodology-world-university-rankings-2019

CHAPTER 10

Impact of Globalization on Higher Education-A Comparative Study Between Public and Private Universities

M.R. Jyothifrederick[1,*]

[1] Goverment Degree College, Narasannapeta, Srikakulam, Dr. Ambedkar University, Srikakulam, India

Abstract: Today, higher education is no more constrained by geographical boundaries. Innovative forms of translocation and transnational education have become a possibility. In India, higher education reforms are emerging in isolated niches in higher education institutions. Globalization has been attracting considerable attention from higher education institutions both in government and private sectors and discussed at national seminars and conferences. The main aim of this study was to find the impact of globalization on higher education. The data is collected from the faculty members of Public and Private Universities and comparative analysis has been done between these two groups. Perceptive score differences were observed between the teaching faculty of GITAM university and Andhra University on the impact of globalization on higher education. Significant differences were found in innovations, quality measures, external exposure, and policy measures. It is also observed that the services of GITAM University are more satisfactory than Andhra University. Whereas the faculty members of Andhra University felt more satisfaction than GITAM University in faculty-related quality measures, external exposure, and policy matters.

Keywords: Autonomy, Distance education, Exposure, GATS, Globalization, Higher Education, Impact, Information technology, Innovation, Learning centers, Multimedia, Private university, Research, Research institutes, Skills, WTO.

INTRODUCTION

Globalization has given a boost to higher education in India by opening horizons of progress in every sector. This globalization has also made distant education available inside the country. The instant impact of it is that students, who are more diligent and meritorious but devoid of resources to avail the latest educational patterns through visiting foreign countries, would get this facility in

---

* **Corresponding author M.R. Jyothifrederick:** Goverment Degree College, Narasannapeta, Srikakulam, Dr. Ambedkar University, Srikakulam, India; Tel: 9505566220; E-mail: jyothifrederick1961@gmail.com

Sankara Narayana Rao Gedala and P.L. Saranya (Eds)
All rights reserved-© 2021 Bentham Science Publishers

India. Multimedia Technology has come into vogue and is becoming popular due to its multidimensional approach and used by this globalization. It has also facilitated and brought leverage in higher education.

The impact of globalization and WTO & GATS on Higher Education would be multidimensional and it would be influenced by the higher education policy, programs, and its implementation. Globalization impacts the very system of higher education, the structure, functions and structure-function relations, as well as the accreditation and assessment of higher education (Nayak, 2015). If higher education becomes a part of the WTO, it necessitates restructuring the higher education system, not only to cater to the new set of international regulations but also to cater to the international market place, which means universities are to guarantee market access to educational products and institutions of all kinds (Sharma, 2013).

Today higher education is no more constrained by geographical boundaries. Innovative forms of translocation and transnational education have become a possibility. Multi-campus institutions, franchised institutions learning centers providing university degree, off-campus education, distance learning, internet-based distance education, virtual universities merging of part studies to combine into a whole for obtaining national as well as international degrees are only a few models examples. As far as higher education is concerned, an enthused and well-informed student has umpteen choices, for the first time in the history of education, to access a global marketplace (Prahalladappa, 2014). With the effect of globalization, all universities, engineering colleges, medical colleges, and other institutions of higher learning, as well as research and development organizations, would be networked for distance education programs to improve the quality of education. Virtual institutes would be set up in different parts of the country for distance education. Various initiatives to promote information technology literacy were indicated, including the program of management studies. Connectivity is coming to universities, and distance education is making available new learning opportunities to the opted students (Sharma, Naveen, 2012).

As far as the quality, access, relevance, and equity of higher education is concerned, little is yet known about the consequences of GATS, as well as the extent of GATS' influence on the national authority to regulate higher education systems, and unforeseen consequences on public subsidies for higher education. There is this fear of the unknown with regard to the impact of WTO and GATS on the Higher Education sector that is haunting the minds of those concerned with higher education in India. Under these circumstances, the so-called India's higher education institutions and their capacity to entice and retain world-class faculty and students in the face of attractive offers from foreign universities, research institutes, and multinational corporations are the main issue. The cream of students, hitherto the prerogative of these higher education institutions, might have to choose among the best. The apprehension that haunts the Indian mind is that universities and students in India might be the losers in the game of global higher education (Shailendra, 2016).

NEED AND SIGNIFICANCE OF THE STUDY

Globalization has a significant impact on Indian higher education, but India's higher education sector has failed to map the future demand for various skills, global competition and competitiveness as higher education system in India suffers from proper administration, acute paucity of funds, lack of autonomy, and burden of affiliation. Moreover, the higher education has been affected by politicization, poor quality of intake, heterogeneity of student population, communication gap between universities and colleges, unsystematic growth of institutions, managerial inefficiencies, overcrowded classroom, wastage in instructional hours, poor course design, inadequate student service, inadequate material resources, inefficiencies in teaching, and lack of training facilities for educational administrators and teachers. Now the students have an easy scope to acquire higher education because a lot of colleges and universities have been opened for higher education. Thus, along with the quantitative expansion of quality in higher education, the government must take some policy measures to improve educational administration standards as well as solve the burgeoning problem of enrollment (Younis Ahmad Sheikh, 2017). Globalization of Higher Education is the need of the hour in a fiercely competitive world, and India cannot lag behind such requirements. While the globalization of Indian higher education is imperative, an in-depth study on the impact of globalization on higher education in India has to be done. In this context, the aspect of globalization in the Indian education system, the growth and development of higher education in India, the recent national education policy need to be studied. This has led to an understanding of the Indian scenario and helped the policy makers in conceptualizing the need to establish new administrative policies in the current higher education system. It encourages international universities to exchange their academic and research knowledge with India. Hence, this paper dealt with the concept of globalization in the Indian higher education system and ensured its effective and comprehensive implementation with a view to positioning India as an educational hub. The objectives of the work is to study the impact of globalization on reforms in Higher Education with reference to services, innovations, quality measures, external exposure, and policy measures and provide a comparison between the impact of globalization on higher education in public and private universities.

METHODOLOGY

Higher Education has experienced a boom with an explosion in the number of Higher Education institutions across the states in India. Andhra Pradesh is one of the wealthiest and potential states in the country, with an unprecedented increase in the number of Higher Education institutions. Over the entire country, the universities and colleges are offering Higher Education to academic scholars. These fall into two categories based on their ownership, where the first one is Government and the second one is Private. Hence this study has considered two higher education institutions *i.e.*, Andhra University and Gandhi Institute of Technology and Management (GITAM) University in Visakhapatnam. In these modern days, where the right to education is imparted to even the lowest category of citizens in India, Higher Education has become a privilege to all, and Globalization in Higher Education has a vast impact. The general public opinion is that the output of Private Universities is better than that of Public Universities in promoting higher education. Hence, in this context, a comparative study on the impact of globalization on higher education with reference to services, innovations, quality measures, external exposure and policy measures have been considered, where the Andhra University of Public Sector and GITAM University of Private Sector have been taken as study units.

Perceptions of the teaching faculty of selected two higher education institutions *i.e.*, Andhra University and GITAM University in Visakhapatnam, have been considered with reference to educational services. For this purpose, primary data collected through a predestinated questionnaire consisted of the impact of globalization on reforms in higher education. Hence, the sample of the study comprises 320 faculty members selected from two universities (68 in Andhra University and 252 in GITAM University, based on their population) from 14 departments which are in both universities. After data collection, an attempt was made to analyze and understand the perceptions of the respondents about the impact of globalization on higher education. The data was processed through SPSS and design tables, and results are analyzed and discussed. Statistical calculations like simple percentages, mean values and rank score analysis were used and t-tests were used for the comparison of the impact of globalization on public and private universities with perceptive scores.

DATA ANALYSIS

This part of data analysis deals with five areas, including 1) Service, 2) Innovations, 3) Quality measures, 4) External exposure, and 5) Policy measures. In each area, there are five statements and the perceptions of respondents on statements have been presented by frequency and percentages and based on the score values, ranks have been given to east statements and presented in the following Table 1.

Table 1. The perception of teaching faculty on service reforms in higher education.

S. No.	Statement	Highly Important	Important	Neutral	Not Important	Not at all Important	Total
-	Scale Value (SV)	5	4	3	2	1	-
1	Appealing and attractive infrastructures	21 (6.6)	71 (22.2)	27 (8.4)	180 (56.3)	21 (6.6)	320 (100.0)
-	Frequency x Scale Value	21	142	81	720	105	1069 –II
2	Students undertake projects in reputed companies	27 (8.4)	78 (24.4)	10 (3.1)	179 (55.9)	26 (8.1)	320 (100.0)
-	Frequency x Scale Value (F X SV)	27	156	30	716	130	1059 – IV
3	Industrial visits & training programs	45 (14.1)	68 (21.3)	6 (1.9)	148 (46.3)	53 (16.6)	320 (100.0)
-	Frequency x Scale Value (F X SV)	45	136	18	592	265	1056 – V
4	Conducting skill development programs	30 (9.4)	71 (22.2)	14 (4.4)	161 (50.3)	44 (13.8)	320 (100.0)
-	Frequency x Scale Value (F X SV)	30	142	42	644	220	1078 – I
5	Conducting of campus interview	23 (7.2)	78 (24.4)	15 (4.7)	176 (55.0)	28 (8.8)	320 (100.0)
-	Frequency x Scale Value (F X SV)	23	156	45	704	140	1068 – III
-	Total score for Services	-	-	-	-	-	5330
-	Maximum Possible Score	5 (Maximum score points) X 320 (number of respondents) X 5 (number of statements)					8000
-	Average score of services in higher education	Total score for Services/Number of Statements					1066

Services

Table **1** represents the perception of teaching faculty related to reform factors of higher education on services. It is noticed that the 1st rank is obtained by the statement 'Conducting of skill development programs' with a scale value of 1078, in that 50.3 percent of the respondents said that it is not important and 4.4 percent of members supposed neutral, 2nd rank is obtained by 'Appealing and attractive infrastructures of the college' with a scale value of 1069 in which more than fifty percent of the respondents *i.e.* 56.3 percent believed that it is not important whereas 6.6 percent thought it is not at all important, 3rd rank is given to 'conducting of campus interview' with a scale value of 1068 from which 55.0 percent of respondents believed that it is not important and 4.7 percent are supposed to be neutral. It is observed that 4th rank is given to 'Colleges helps students undertake projects in reputed companies' with a scale value of 1059 in that 55.9 percent of them said that it is not important and 3.1 are supposed to be neutral, 5th rank is given to 'Industry relevant programs offered by the college (Industrial Training Programs & Industrial Visits)' with a scale value of 1056 in which 46.3 percent believed that it is not important whereas 1.9 percent of the respondents are neutral.

As per the above information, it is concluded that 'Conducting of skill development programs', 'Appealing and attractive infrastructures of the college' and 'Conducting of campus interview' are higher than the average value *i.e.*, 1066, whereas remaining statements 'Colleges helps students undertake projects in reputed companies' and 'Industry relevant programs offered by the college (Industrial Training Programs & Industrial Visits)' are found to be lower than the average value and these are obtained to be negative sense among the sample faculty members.

Innovations

Table **2** shows the perception of teaching faculty related to reform factors of higher education on innovations. The 1st rank is given to the statement 'Implementation of advanced technology in teaching methods have been adopted' with a scale value of 852 from which 45.0 percent of the respondents said that it is not important whereas 5.6 percent have a neutral opinion, 2nd rank is given to 'Courses in Soft Skills/Personality Development Programs offered by the college' with a scale value of 845, in that 46.3 percent believed that it is not important and 7.5 percent have a neutral opinion, 3rd rank is given to 'Innovative Teaching/Learning Methods like Smart classrooms, Audiovisual & Computer based modes followed by the college' with a scale value of 842 from that 45.9 percent said that it is not important whereas 6.9 percent have a neutral opinion. It is found that 4th rank is given to 'Innovative Course Curriculum offered by the college' with a scale value of 824 in that nearly fifty percent of respondents, *i.e.* 48.8 percent, said that it is not important whereas 8.1 percent believed that it is highly important, 5th rank is given to 'Modern Labs, internet, Libraries, Wi-Fi

Environment like facilities available in the campus' with a scale value of 817 from which nearly fifty percent, *i.e.* 49.4 percent, said that it is not important whereas 8.4 percent believed that it is highly important. The total percentage of the score of reform factors of higher education on innovations is 52.2 percent.

Table 2. The perception of teaching faculty on innovation reforms in higher education.

S. No.	Statement	Highly Important	Important	Neutral	Not Important	Not at all Important	Total
-	Scale Value (SV)	5	4	3	2	1	-
1	Innovative Course Curriculum offered by the college	26 (8.1)	62 (19.4)	29 (9.1)	156 (48.8)	47 (14.7)	320 (100.0)
-	Frequency x Scale Value	130	248	87	312	47	824 – IV
2	Courses in Soft Skills/Personality Development Programs	29 (9.1)	71 (22.2)	24 (7.5)	148 (46.3)	48 (15.0)	320 (100.0)
-	Frequency x Scale Value	145	284	72	296	48	845 –II
3	Availability of modern Labs, internet, libraries, Wi-Fi facilities	27 (8.4)	57 (17.8)	30 (9.4)	158 (49.4)	48 (15.0)	320 (100.0)
-	Frequency x Scale Value	135	228	90	316	48	817 – V
4	Innovative Teaching/Learning Methods	25 (7.8)	77 (24.1)	22 (6.9)	147 (45.9)	49 (15.3)	320 (100.0)
-	Frequency x Scale Value	125	308	66	294	49	842 – III
5	Implementation of advanced technology in teaching methods have been adopted	31 (9.7)	76 (23.8)	18 (5.6)	144 (45.0)	51 (15.9)	320 (100.0)
-	Frequency x Scale Value	155	304	54	288	51	852 – I
-	Total score for Innovations	-	-	-	-	-	4180
-	Maximum Possible Score	5 (Maximum score points) X 320 (number of respondents) X 5 (number of statements)					8000
-	Average score of innovations in higher education	Total score for Services/Number of Statements					836

According to the above analysis, it is concluded that 'Implementation of advanced technology in teaching methods have been adopted', 'Courses in Soft

Skills/Personality Development Programs offered by the college' and 'Innovative Teaching/Learning Methods like Smart class Rooms, Audiovisual & Computer based modes followed by the college' are considered to be greater than average value *i.e.,* 836. On the contrary, remaining statements 'Innovative Course Curriculum offered by the college' and 'Modern Labs, internet, Libraries, Wi-Fi Environment like facilities available in the campus' are found to be less than average value and these are obtained to be negative among the sample faculty members.

Table 3 represents the perception of teaching faculty related to reform factors of higher education on quality measures. It is observed that 'Qualified Faculty of the college' this statement got 1st rank with a scale value of 896 in that 37.5 percent of people said that it is not important whereas 6.6 percent have a neutral opinion, 2nd rank is given to 'Scholarships offered by the college to meritorious students' with a scale value of 892 from which 41.3 percent supposed that it is not important and 6.9 percent are supposedly neutral, 3rd rank is obtained by 'On/Off campus recruitment activity carried out in the college' based on the scale value 886 in that 33.1 percent said that it is not important whereas 3.4 percent have a neutral opinion. It is noticed that 4th rank is given to 'Intimation to parents regarding students academic reports' with a scale value of 869 from that 43.4 percent of respondents said that it is not important and 3.1 percent have a neutral opinion on that, 5th rank is obtained by 'Reasonable fees collected from the students' with a scale value of 853 from which 34.4 percent believed that it is not important and 11.3. percent have neutral opinions. The total percentage of score of reform factors of higher education on quality measures is 54.9 percent.

Table 3. Perception of teaching faculty on quality measure reforms in higher education.

S. No.	Statement	Highly Important	Important	Neutral	Not Important	Not at all Important	Total
-	Scale Value (SV)	5	4	3	2	1	-
1	Qualified Faculty of the college	33 (10.3)	94 (29.4)	21 (6.6)	120 (37.5)	52 (16.3)	320 (100.0)
-	Frequency x Scale Value	165	376	63	240	52	896-I
2	Intimation to parents regarding students academic reports	39 (12.2)	78 (24.4)	10 (3.1)	139 (43.4)	54 (16.9)	320 (100.0)

106 Assessment, Accreditation and Ranking Methods for Higher Education   M.R. Jyothifrederick

(Table 3) cont.....

S. No.	Statement	Highly Important	Important	Neutral	Not Important	Not at all Important	Total
-	Frequency x Scale Value	195	312	30	278	54	869-IV
3	On/Off campus recruitment activity carried out in the college	51 (15.9)	78 (24.4)	11 (3.4)	106 (33.1)	74 (23.1)	320 (100.0)
-	Frequency x Scale Value	255	312	33	212	74	886-III
4	Reasonable fees collected from the students	39 (12.2)	65 (20.3)	36 (11.3)	110 (34.4)	70 (21.9)	320 (100.0)
320 (100.0) 48 (15.0) 132 (41.3) 22 (6.9) 76 (23.8) 42 (13.1)	Frequency x Scale Value	195	260	108	220	70	853-V
5	Scholarships offered by the college to meritorious students						
	Frequency x Scale Value	210	304	66	264	48	892-II
-	Total score for Quality measures	-	-	-	-	-	4396
-	Maximum Possible Score	5 (Maximum score points) X 320 (number of respondents) X 5 (number of statements)					8000
-	Average score of quality measures in higher education	Total score for Services/Number of Statements					879

Quality Measures

As per the above information, it is concluded that 'Qualified Faculty of the college', 'Scholarships offered by the college to meritorious students' and 'On/Off campus recruitment activity carried out in the college' are considered to be greater than the average value, *i.e.*, 879. On the other hand, 'Intimation to parents regarding students academic reports' and 'Reasonable fees collected from the students' are found to be less than the average value and these are obtained to be negative among the sample faculty respondents.

Table 4. Perception of teaching faculty on external exposure reforms in higher education.

S. No.	Statement	Highly Important	Important	Neutral	Not Important	Not at all Important	Total
-	Scale Value (SV)	5	4	3	2	1	-
1	Institutions clinch with corporate sectors	34 (10.6)	50 (15.6)	33 (10.3)	141 (4.1)	62 (19.4)	320 (100.0)
-	Frequency x Scale Value	170	200	99	282	62	813 – II
2	Visiting of faculty from top ranking corporate institutions & IIT's	32 (10.0)	64 (20.0)	29 (9.1)	141 (44.1)	54 (16.9)	320 (100.0)
-	Frequency x Scale Value	160	256	87	282	54	839 – I
3	Collaboration with reputed educational institutions	31 (9.7)	50 (15.6)	9 (2.8)	142 (44.4)	88 (27.5)	320 (100.0)
-	Frequency x Scale Value	155	200	27	284	88	754 – V
4	Induction of modern academic teaching and research methodologies	35 (10.9)	50 (15.6)	21 (6.6)	119 (37.2)	95 (29.7)	320 (100.0)
-	Frequency x Scale Value	175	200	63	238	95	771 – IV
5	Reorientation of Research Innovations	26 (8.1)	50 (15.6)	24 (7.5)	159 (49.7)	61 (19.1)	320 (100.0)
-	Frequency x Scale Value	130	200	72	318	61	781 – III
-	Total score for External Exposure	-	-	-	-	-	3958
-	Maximum Possible Score	5 (Maximum score points) X 320 (number of respondents) X 5 (number of statements)					8000
-	Average score of external exposure in higher education	Total score for Services/Number of Statements					791

External Exposure

Table 4 represents the perception of teaching faculty related to reform factors of higher education on external exposure. It is noticed that 1st rank is given to the statement 'Visiting of faculty from top ranking corporate institutions &

IIT's/executives from Industries to deliver guest lectures' with a scale value of 839 in which 44.1 percent of respondents said that it is not important whereas 9.1 percent of them have a neutral opinion, 2nd rank is given to 'Institutions clinch with corporate sectors' with a scale value of 813 in which 19.4 percent said that it is not at all important whereas 4.1 percent said that it is not important. It is found that the 3rd rank is given to 'Reorientation of Research Innovations' with a scale value of 781 from that nearly fifty percent of them *i.e.*, 49.7 percent thought it is not important whereas 7.5 percent have a neutral opinion, 4th rank is given to 'Induction of modern academic teaching and research methodologies' with a scale value of 771 in which 37.2 percent believed that it is not important whereas 6.6 percent have a neutral opinion, 5th rank is given to 'Collaboration with reputed educational institutions' with a scale value of 754 from that 44.4 percent said that it is not important and 2.8 percent have a neutral opinion. The total percentage of the score of reform factors of higher education on external exposure is 49.4 percent.

According to the above analysis, it is concluded that the statements 'Visiting faculty from top ranking corporate institutions & IIT's/executives from Industries to deliver guest lectures' and 'Institutions clinch with corporate sectors' are found to be greater than average value, *i.e.*, 791. On the contrary, remaining statements 'Reorientation of Research Innovations', 'Induction of modern academic teaching and research methodologies' and 'Collaboration with reputed educational institutions' are less than average value and are obtained to be negative among all the sample faculty members.

Table 5. Perception of teaching faculty on policy measure reforms in higher education.

S. No.	Statement	Highly Important	Important	Neutral	Not Important	Not at all Important	Total
-	Scale Value (SV)	5	4	3	2	1	-
1	Quality assurance in Higher Education	46 (14.4)	49 (15.3)	29 (9.1)	143 (44.7)	53 (16.6)	320 (100.0)
-	Frequency x Scale Value	230	196	87	286	53	852 – III
2	Financial investment in Higher Education	41 (12.8)	83 (25.9)	18 (5.6)	129 (40.3)	49 (15.3)	320 (100.0)
-	Frequency x Scale Value	205	332	54	258	49	898 – I
3	Implementation and monitoring of National Education Policy	33 (10.3)	51 (15.9)	48 (15.0)	136 (42.5)	52 (16.3)	320 (100.0)
-	Frequency x Scale Value	165	204	144	272	52	837 – IV

S. No.	Statement	Highly Important	Important	Neutral	Not Important	Not at all Important	Total
4	Identify new knowledge domains	47 (14.7)	60 (18.8)	33 (10.3)	101 (31.6)	79 (24.7)	320 (100.0)
-	Frequency x Scale Value	235	240	99	202	79	855 – II
5	Internationalization of education system	33 (10.3)	27 (8.4)	21 (6.6)	157 (49.1)	82 (25.6)	320 (100.0)
-	Frequency x Scale Value	165	108	63	314	82	732 – V
-	Total score for Policy Measures	-	-	-	-	-	4174
-	Maximum Possible Score	5 (Maximum score points) X 320 (number of respondents) X 5 (number of statements)					8000
-	Average score of policy measures in higher education	Total score for Services/Number of Statements					834

Policy Measures

Table 5 signifies that the perception of teaching faculty related to reform factors of higher education on policy measures. It is noticed that 1st rank is given to the statement 'Financial investment in Higher Education' with a scale value of 898 from that 40.3 percent of respondents said that it is not important whereas 5.6 percent have a neutral opinion, 2nd rank is given to 'Identify new knowledge domains (pedagogy, curricular and assessment reforms)' with a scale value of 855 in that 31.6 percent thought it is not important whereas 10.3 percent have a neutral opinion, 3rd rank is obtained by 'Quality assurance in Higher Education' with a scale value of 852 from that 44.7 percent of them believed that it is not important whereas 9.1 percent have a neutral opinion. It is observed that 4th rank is given to 'Implementation and monitoring of National Education Policy' with a scale value of 837 from which 42.5 percent said that it is not important whereas 10.3 percent thought that is highly important, 5th rank is given to 'Internationalization of education system (foreign degrees in collaboration with Indian universities' with a scale value of 732 in that 49.1 percent of respondents said that it is not important whereas 6.6 percent have a neutral opinion. The total percentage of the score of reform factors of higher education on policy measures is 52.1 percent.

As per the above information, it is concluded that 'Financial investment in Higher Education', 'Identify new knowledge domains (pedagogy, curricular and assessment reforms)', 'Quality assurance in Higher Education' and 'Implementation and monitoring of National Education Policy' are greater than average value, *i.e.*, 834. On the other hand, the remaining statements

'Internationalization of education system (foreign degrees in collaboration with Indian universities) is found to be less than average value and it is obtained to be negative among all the sample faculty members.

Table 6. Perceptive score difference between faculty members of GITAM and Andhra Universities on the impact of globalization on higher education.

Statement	University	N	Mean	Std. Dev	Std. Error	t-value	P-value
Services	GITAM University	252	14.44	5.79	0.37	12.948	0.000**
	Andhra University	68	9.28	1.33	0.16		
Innovations	GITAM University	252	14.14	5.89	0.37	12.243	0.000**
	Andhra University	68	9.07	1.51	0.18		
Quality measures	GITAM University	252	13.02	4.38	0.28	6.214	0.000**
	Andhra University	68	16.40	3.86	0.47		
External Exposure	GITAM University	252	11.98	4.08	0.26	3.683	0.000**
	Andhra University	68	13.79	3.45	0.42		
Policy Measures	GITAM University	252	12.69	3.51	0.22	3.198	0.002**
	Andhra University	68	14.34	3.83	0.46		

** Significant @ 1%.

Table 6 represents the perceptive score difference between the universities of globalization on education policies in higher education. It is noticed that in the globalization impact on the education system the mean value of Andhra University members, *i.e.*, 20.38, which is higher than that of GITAM University (18.62). The calculated t-value is 4.706, which are significant at one percent level as the p-value 0.000 is less than 0.01. This shows that Andhra University members are more positive towards the globalization impact on the education system. It is observed that the higher education at Andhra University was found to be higher with a mean value of 20.34 and GITAM University with a mean value of 17.76. The calculated t-value is 7.163, which are found significant at one percent level as the p-value 0.000 is less than 0.01. This indicates that Andhra University members are more positive towards the present scenario of higher education. As per the services, it was found that the average score of GITAM University is higher *i.e.* 14.44 than the Andhra University mean score *i.e.*, 9.28. The calculated t-value is 12.948, which are significant at one percent level as the p-value 0.000 is less than 0.001. Therefore it is observed that at services, GITAM University was found to be more satisfying. Regarding the innovations, it is noticed that the average mean value of GITAM University is 14.14, which is higher than the average score value of Andhra University (9.07). The calculated t-value is 12.234, which is significant at one percent level as the p-value 0.000 is less than 0.01. This says that the innovations at GITAM University are more positive.

From the quality measures, it is found that the Andhra University's average score is higher, *i.e.*, 16.40, than the GITAM University average score (13.02). The calculated t-value is 6.214 is found to be significant at one percent level as the p-value 0.000 is less than 0.01. This shows that from the quality measures, Andhra University is highly satisfied.

It is noticed that the average score value of Andhra University members in external exposures is 13.79, which is higher than the average score of GITAM University people (11.98). The calculated t-value is 3.683 which are significant at one percent level as the p-value 0.000 is less than 0.001. Therefore this shows that Andhra University members are highly satisfied with the external exposures. According to the policy measures, it is noticed that the average score value of Andhra University (14.34) is higher than the GITAM University (12.69). While the calculated t-value 3.198 was found to be significant at one percent level, the p-value 0.002 is less than 0.01. This indicates that most of the members of Andhra University are more satisfied.

MAJOR FINDINGS

The perceptional scores of teaching faculty related to the reform of higher education on services shows that 'Conducting skill development programs', 'Appealing and attractive infrastructures of the college' and 'campus placements' are found to be higher than the average score value *i.e.*, 1066, whereas 'Colleges helps students undertake projects in reputed companies' and 'Industry relevant programs offered by the college (Industrial Training Programs & Industrial Visits)' are found less than the average score value. The perception score of teaching faculty related to innovations reform in higher education shows that 'Implementation of advanced technology in teaching methods have been adopted', 'Courses in Soft Skills/Personality Development Programs offered by the college' and 'Innovative Teaching/Learning Methods like Smart class Rooms, Audiovisual & Computer based modes followed by the college' are considered to be more positive where the score value is higher than the average (836). On the contrary, 'Innovative Course Curriculum offered by the college' and 'Modern Labs, internet, Libraries, Wi-Fi Environment like facilities available in the campus' are found to be less than the average score and these are obtained to have a negative sense of impact on globalization. The data reveals from the perception of teaching faculty on reform of quality measures in higher education shows that 'Qualified Faculty of the college', 'Scholarships offered by the college to meritorious students' and 'On/Off campus recruitment activity carried out in the college' are considered to be more satisfactory with high score than average (879). On the other hand 'Intimation to parents regarding students academic reports' and 'Reasonable fees collected from the students' are found to be less satisfied with less average score sensing negative impression among the faculty members. Perceptional score of teaching faculty related to external exposure reforms in higher education shows that 'Visiting of faculty from top ranking corporate institutions & IIT's/executives from Industries to deliver guest lectures' and 'Institutions clinch with corporate sectors' are found to be more satisfied than 'Reorientation of Research Innovations', 'Induction of modern academic teaching and research methodologies' and 'Collaboration with reputed educational institutions', where the mean score indicate 791. As per the data the perception of teaching faculty towards reform of policy measures in higher education found that 'Financial investment in Higher Education', 'Identify new knowledge domains (pedagogy, curricular and assessment reforms)', 'Quality assurance in Higher Education' and 'Implementation and monitoring of National Education Policy' are higher satisfaction than the average (834), whereas, 'Internationalization of education system (foreign degrees in collaboration with Indian universities' is found less satisfaction than the average among the faculty members. Perceptive score difference between the GITAM university and Andhra University teaching faculty on impact of globalization on higher education shows that there is a significant difference between these two groups in globalization impact on education system, higher education at present scenario, innovations, quality measures, external exposure, policy measures, privatization and commercialization of higher education and reservation policy and impact of globalization on external process and national policy on higher education. It is also observed that in the impact of globalization on higher education services, innovation and reservation policies the GITAM university faculty members are more positive than Andhra University members. Whereas in globalization impact on education system, Higher education at present scenario, quality measures, external exposure, policy measures, privatization and commercialization of higher education, impact of globalization on enrollment process and impact of national policies on higher education the Andhra University faculty members are more positive than the GITAM university.

The survey helps the public Universities to re-look into their policies and framework for offering better education services to stakeholders. It provides insight to the private Universities in the area of academic and Career satisfaction of the faculty for improving performance in the ranking.

CONCLUSION

In India, higher education reforms are emerging in isolated niches in higher education institutions. We have to acknowledge that globalization is a driving force for national development that attempts to modify institutions and bring them in line with progress. It is essential that India embraces an aggressive, result-oriented approach for being consistent with the global developments in the higher education sector. Globalization has been attracting considerable attention from higher education institutions both in government and private sectors and discussed at national seminars and conferences. For the Indian higher education sector, globalization process is an exploring stage. The domestic institutions (both government and private) are judging the feasibility of exporting higher education by creating tie-ups, franchisees, and alliances either with private or international providers in the global market. The research revealed that in the coming decade, international academic exchange, increased cross-cultural linkages will enrich the domestic knowledge sphere. Internationalization of higher education services will increase the flow of funds and resources for the improvement of the infrastructure of present domestic institutes. Competition will put forward the challenges as achieving maximum efficiency, reduction in cost, and raising revenue resources since fittest survival quality improvement will take place as an outcome of foreign competition and a reduction in protection measures.

CONSENT FOR PUBLICATION

Not applicable.

CONFLICT OF INTEREST

The author declares no conflict of interest, financial or otherwise.

ACKNOWLEDGEMENTS

Declared none.

REFERENCES

Naik, P. K. (2015). Globalization and its impact on higher education in India. *International Journal of Humanities and Management Sciences (IJHMS)*, 3(6), 2320-4044. http://www.isaet.org/images/extraimages/UH0116002.pdf

Prahalladappa, M.H. (2014). Globalization and higher education in India: a world in one nest. *Voice of Research*, 2(4), 2277-7333. http://www.voiceofresearch.org/Doc/Mar-2014/Mar-2014_10.pdf

Sharma, N. (2012). Globalization effect on education and culture. *Analysis*, (May), 28. [http://dx.doi.org/10.2139/ssrn.2069155]

Sharma, S.N. (2013). *Management Studies – Exploring New Opportunities.*. New Delhi, India: Edupedia Publications Pvt. Ltd..

Sheikh, Y.A. (2017). Higher education in India: challenges and opportunities. *J. Educ. Pract.*, 8(1), 2017. https://files.eric.ed.gov/fulltext/EJ1131773.pdf

Singh, S. (2016). Impact of globalization on higher education in India: issues, challenges and alternatives. *The International J Indian Psychology,* *3*(2). http://oaji.net/articles/ 2016/1170-1453808995.pdf

CHAPTER 11

Challenges and Prospects of Higher Education in India

Smt. M. Santhi[1] and Smt. T. Adilakshmi[1,*]

[1] Deptartment of Economics, Govt. College for Women (A) Srikakulam, Dr. Ambedkar University, Srikakulam, India

Abstract: Today the concept of economic development plays a vital role in worldwide nations. The development of any economy mainly depends upon the availability and utilisation of Technology, Capital Accumulation, Natural and Human Resources. Besides other factors, human resources are particularly important for economic development. Hence the government should focus on factors like quality education (both primary & higher education), proper training, skills and health care for human resource development. In this context, this paper tried to analyze the importance of higher education in economic development, the present scenario and growth of higher education institutions in India, the problems that the higher education institutions are facing today at the college and university level, the challenges that are to be addressed and the prospects of higher education in India. The methodology used in the paper is mainly qualitative in nature, and secondary sources like, Economic Survey, AISHE reports are being used to acquire sufficient data to analyze the situation of higher education in India.

Keywords: Availability, Capital Accumulation, Challenges, College, Economic Development, Factors, Health care, Higher Education, Human Resource, Institutions, Instruments, Natural Resources, Population, Problems, Productive, Prospects, Qualitative, Technology, Training, University.

INTRODUCTION

Today all the countries in the world are focused on economic growth and development. It is possible through the availability and utilization of technology, capital accumulation, natural resources, and, more importantly, human resources. Higher education plays a very important role in economic development through the development of human resources. Simply we can say that economic and social development took place, where the higher education system developed. The 20th and 21st centuries have witnessed the role of higher education in sustainable, eco-

---

[*] **Corresponding author Smt. T. Adilakshmi:** Deptartment of Economics, Govt. College for Women (A) Srikakulam, Dr Ambedkar University, Srikakulam, India; Tel: 7989684463; E-mail: adilaxmi1987@gmail.com

Sankara Narayana Rao Gedala and P.L. Saranya (Eds)
All rights reserved-© 2021 Bentham Science Publishers

nomic development. It creates high wage employment opportunities, increases productivity, production, the standard of living and the quality of lives of human beings, and also it is very important for acquiring new knowledge, research and its application. It makes a great contribution to economic development through fostering skill training, research and innovations. We can say that it plays a paramount role in improving the quality of life and addressing major economic, social and global challenges. Hence it is considered one of the key drivers of economic development, prosperity and competitiveness.

India, as the 2nd largest populated country after China, needs more investment in human capital. It is a prerequisite for a healthy and productive population for national building (Economic Survey-2017-18) and to reap the benefit of the demographic dividend. Hence it is essential to invest in education, especially in higher education. India's education system is the 3rd largest in size after China and U.S.A. in the world (Sharma. S & Sharma. P. 2015), and it has traveled a long way from ancient time to the modern age. Ancient history records tell us that India has a well developed system of higher education in line with the modern university process. Takshashila, Nalanda and Vikramasila, the prominent universities in the world were running in ancient India during the 6th century B.C and 4th and 5th centuries AD respectively. During the medieval period the Muslims established institutions of higher learning which were known as Madarsas and later on modern higher educational institutions were established during the British period and these modern educational institutions have been continued till today with some changes in the course of time.

The involvement of the private sector in higher education has seen drastic changes in the field (Younis Y.S, 20170), about 39% of the universities and 78% of the colleges are run by the private sector leading to the establishment of more number of universities and colleges during the last three decades. If we observe the growth pattern of the number of universities and colleges listed on AISHE portal (AISHE -2011, 2019) during 2010-11 to 2018-19, we inferred that, the number of universities has increased from 621 in 2010-11 to 993 in 2018-19 by almost 59.9% as shown in Fig. (**1**). Whereas the number of colleges has increased from 32974 in 2010-11 to 39,931 in 2018-19 by about 21.09%, as shown in Fig. (**2**). That means the percentage of universities increased more than that of the colleges. Hence the government should identify the states and districts which are having less number of colleges and universities and increase them to provide higher educational opportunities to the growing younger population.

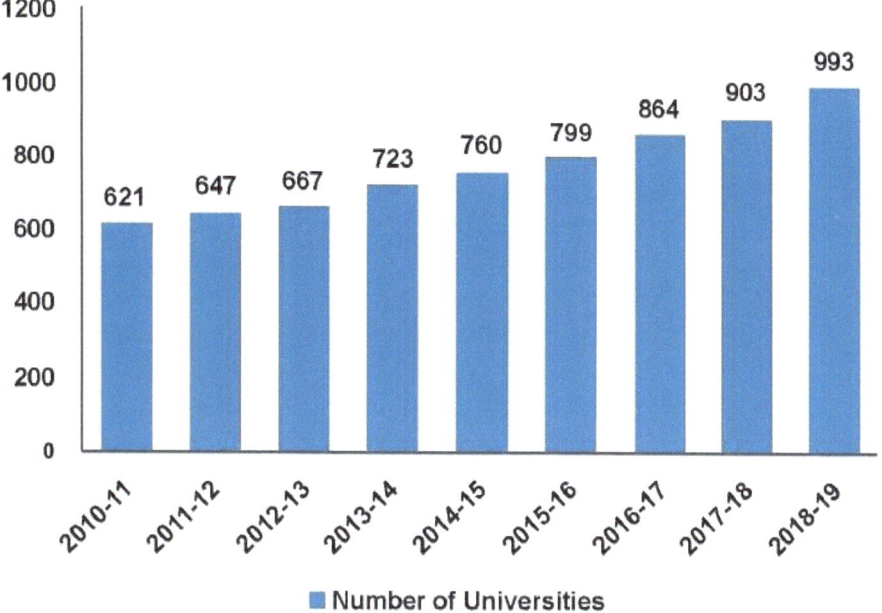

Fig. (1). No. of Universities.

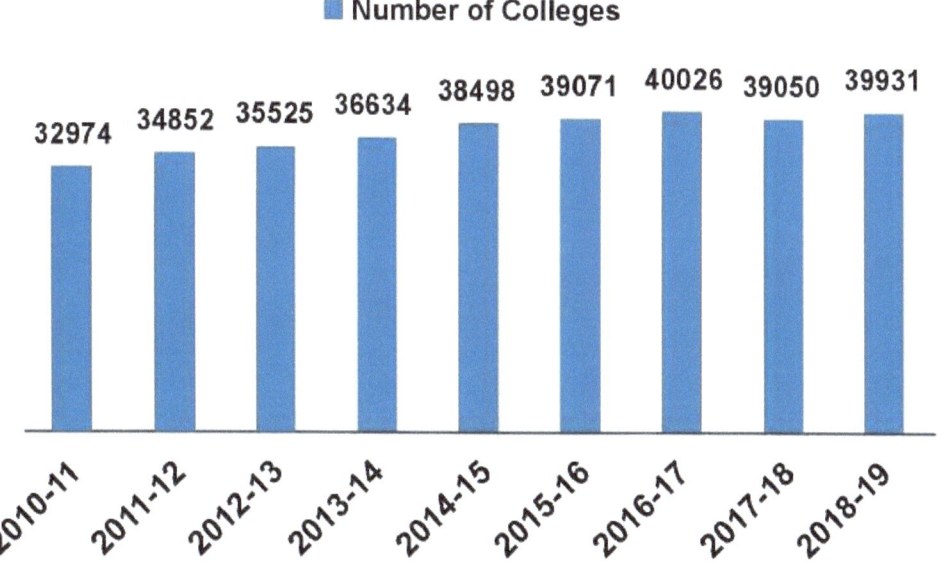

Fig. (2). No. of Colleges.

PRESENT SCENARIO OF HIGHER EDUCATION SYSTEM IN INDIA

The Higher Education system includes universities, colleges and vocational schools, which promote higher learning, research, innovation, entrepreneurship, addressing problems of the society and help the individuals in building their career. Hence the higher education system plays a very important role in shaping our future. According to the latest report on the All India Survey on Higher Education (AISHE, 2019), there are 993 universities, 39931 colleges and 10725 stand-alone institutions in India. Out of 993 universities, 385 (38.77%) are privately managed and 394 (39.67%) are located in rural areas. 16 (1.61%) universities are exclusively for women, 3 in Rajasthan, 2 in Tamil Nadu and 1 each in Andhra Pradesh, Assam, Bihar, Delhi, Haryana, Himachal Pradesh, Karnataka, Maharashtra, Odisha, Uttarakhand and West Bengal.

The above statistics show the need to increase the number of universities located in rural areas to attract the rural students towards higher education and the number of women universities in proportion to the women population to ensure gender equality in higher education and to make women more empowered.

Out of 39931 colleges, 60.53% colleges are located in rural areas and the remaining 39.47% are in urban areas. 11.04% colleges are exclusively for women. 77.8% colleges are privately managed 64.3% private-unaided and 13.5% private-aided. Andhra Pradesh & Uttar Pradesh have about 88% private-unaided colleges and Tamil Nadu has 87% private-unaided colleges, whereas Assam has 16.0%. 2.5% colleges run Ph.D. programs and 34.9% colleges run Post Graduate programs. There are 34.8% colleges, which run only a single program, out of which 83.1% are privately managed. Among these privately managed colleges, 38.1% colleges run B.Ed. courses only. The top 8 states in terms of the highest number of colleges in India are Uttar Pradesh, Maharashtra, Karnataka, Rajasthan, Haryana, Tamil Nadu, Gujarat and Madhya Pradesh, and Bangalore urban district tops in terms of the number of colleges with 880 colleges followed by Jaipur with 566 colleges. Top 50 districts throughout India have about 32.2% of colleges out of 39931 total colleges. This indicates that most of the colleges are owned by the private sector and they are running single programs and only 2.5% colleges run Ph.D. level programs. This indicates negligence of research at the college level and not only that, out of total 39931 colleges, 12857 colleges are located in the top 50 districts of the country, which shows the concentration of educational institutions is high in some areas and other areas being neglected due to many reasons. Hence the governments of these states should focus on these districts to achieve regional educational development and balance.

The total stand-alone institutions are 10725, out of which, 75.5% institutions are mainly run by the private sector; private unaided – 66.20% and Private aided – 9.30%. Only 24.5% institutions are in the government sector, and 56.2% institutions are located in rural areas. These stand-alone institutions are classified into 7 categories as: 1. Diploma Level Technical Institutes recognized by All India Council for Technical Education (AICTE) and administered by State Directorate of Technical Education. 2. Diploma Level Teacher Training Institutes including, District Institute of Education and Training (DIETs) recognized by National Council for Teacher Education (NCTE) and generally administered by State Council for Education Research and Training (SCERT). 3. Diploma Level Nursing Institutes recognized by Indian Nursing Council (INC) and generally administered by State Nursing Council/Boards. 4. PGDM (Post Graduate Diploma in Management) Institutes recognized by AICTE. 5. Institutes directly under the control of various Central Ministries. 6. Para Medical 7. Hotel Management and Catering.

Among all categories of stand-alone institutions, government institutions account for only 24.5% and the remaining institutions are in the private sector. Courses offered in some of these institutions require a huge amount of fee compared to other traditional courses; hence most of the students from poor economic backgrounds may not choose their career in these areas. So, in order to enhance the employment opportunities of lower-middle income groups students and thereby to reduce poverty, income inequalities, the institutions run by the government should increase in the future.

If we observe the student enrollment at the higher education level, it has been estimated to be 37.4 million with 19.2 million males and 18.2 million females. Female constitutes 48.6% of the total enrollment; distance enrollment constitutes about 10.62% of the total enrollment in higher education, of which 44.15% are female students. The total student enrollment has grown significantly during the last 5 years, which has increased from 3,42,11,673 in 2014-15 to 3,73,99,388 in 2018-19 with 9.3% of overall growth (AISHE, 2019) as shown in Fig. (**3**) and the level-wise, total enrollment for the same period can be observed from Table **1**. And it is inferred that, the growth of total enrollment for Ph.D level was about 44.2%, M.Phil -8%, Post Graduation 4.9%, Under Graduation, 9.8%, PG Diploma,4.3%, Diploma 7.6%, Certificate, -4.4%, Integrated 69.9%. The total enrollment of Ph.D and integrated level programs increased drastically and PG Diploma, Diploma, Post Graduation, Under Graduation programs registered significant growth during 2010-11 to 2018-19, but M.Phil, Certificate programs registered negative growth.

Table 1. Level-Wise Enrolment.

Year	Ph.D	M.Phil	Post Graduate	Under Graduate	PG Diploma	Diploma	Certificate	Integrated	Grand Total
2014-15	117301	33371	3853438	27172346	215372	2507694	170245	141870	34211637
2015-16	126451	42523	3917156	27420450	229559	2549160	144060	155422	34584781
2016-17	141037	43267	4007570	28348197	213051	2612209	166617	173957	35705905
2017-18	161412	34109	4114310	29016350	235263	2707934	177223	195777	36642378
2018-19	169170	30692	4042522	29829075	224711	2699395	162697	241126	37399388

India's Gross Enrollment Ratio (GER) in higher education is 26.3%, which is calculated for 18-23 years of age group; and the GER for the male population is 26.3%, for females, it is 26.4%, for Scheduled Castes, it is 23% and for Scheduled Tribes, it is 17.2%. That means it is very low when compared to the national GER of 26.3%. In general, 16.3% of the colleges have enrollment of less than 100 and only 4% colleges have an enrollment of more than 3000, and the estimated GER is quite low as compared to the developed countries. In order to increase GER in all categories of higher education to cope up with existing demand and supply, the government needs to focus on the reasons that lead to low GER at different levels of educational institutions and to solve the problems existing there.

If we look at the Pupil Teacher Ratio (PTR) in universities and colleges, it is 29 if regular mode enrollment is considered, whereas PTR in universities and its constituent units is 18 for regular mode. Though PTR in universities and its constituent units is a good indicator, some states like Bihar, Uttar Pradesh and Jharkhand have more than 50 and which shows more attention should be given to these states to improve quality in higher education and not only that, if PTR considered for subject wise at higher level education it will be more than 40 in all states. To increase the quality of education, it is necessary to identify student strength and actual workload at the end of every year and accordingly take regular faculty/staff appointments in all subjects as per the need at the beginning of the academic year.

In case of student out-turn in different programs; B.A. degree has been awarded to 19.99 lakh students, which is the highest among all programs, with the percentage of male as 42.55% and female as 57.4%. B.Sc. is the second highest with 10.41 lakh students, followed by B.Com. (9.65 lakh). B.Ed. and B.Tech. degrees are awarded to 5.08 lakh and 4.27 lakh students, respectively. 51283 students have been awarded with an M.B.B.S. degree and out of which 26978 are female. At the postgraduate level, the number of students awarded M.A is maximum (5.96 lakh) followed by M.Sc. (2.78 lakhs) and M.B.A. (2.00 lakhs). About 55,380 and

16,691 students have been awarded M.Tech. and M.E. degree, in which the share of male students is more than 61.1% and 52.04%, respectively. 40,813 students were awarded Ph.D. level degrees in 2018, consisting of 23,765 males and 17,048 females. At the Ph.D. level, the maximum number of students out-turn is observed in the science stream (10023), followed by Engineering &Technology (7160). On the other hand, the maximum students out-turn is observed at the PG level in Social Sciences (2.75 lakh) and followed by management with 2.17 lakhs students (AISHE, 2019).

The share of Ph.D. students is the highest in State Public University (34.3%) followed by Institute of National Importance (21.6%), Deemed University-Private (21.6%) and State Private University (13.4%). The share of female students is lowest in the Institutions of National Importance followed by State Private Open Universities, Deemed Universities-Government. The maximum number of students at UG level and PG level is in the arts stream, followed by science, commerce and management. But at Ph.D level program, maximum number of students out-turn is in the science stream followed by Engineering and Technology. This shows research in social sciences and management studies is being neglected. Hence this is the time to focus on research in the social sciences to build harmony in society. The administrators of universities and research institutions have to prepare a plan and allocate funds to motivate and attract the students in these areas of research.

PROBLEMS AND CHALLENGES OF HIGHER EDUCATION SYSTEM IN INDIA

Before the independence, the British government established educational institutions in India only to cater their business needs; later, the government of India recognized the importance of education and its quality in economic development. UGC was established on 28th December, 1953 to strengthen the educational institutions and later it was converted into a statutory body in November, 1956 by the enactment of UGC act 1956 and The Ministry of Human Resource Development (MHRD) was also created on 26th, September in 1985, through the 174th amendment to the Government of India (Allocation of Business) rules 1961 to oversee the higher education system in India. Both UGC and MHRD have been working and monitoring the educational institutions at all levels and focusing on improvement of quality in the higher education sector in India. Even after the completion of more than 7 decades of independence, still, the Indian education system has not been developed to fulfill the objectives of the country. In spite of all the efforts of our government, we are unable to list a single university in the top 100 universities of the world due to many problems, which are discussed below: Gross Enrollment Ratio (GER); is a major problem in higher education in India. It is 26.3%, which is calculated for 18-23 years of age group in 2018-19 (male 26.3%, female 26.4%), which is less by 3.7% as against the UGC target of 30% by 2020. If we compare GER of different countries like China: 39.39% (male 36.56%, female 42.53%), as of 2014, Japan: 63.36% (male 65.73%, female 60.88%) Korea: 95.34% (male 107.84%, female 81.27%) (as of 2013) and the U.S.A.: 86.66% (male 73.47%, female 100.70%) as of 2014 (Higher Education Policy and Development in Asia, 2017) and which is quite low. It has become a major challenge to the government to increase GER given the socioeconomic conditions of the population. Hence the government should allocate sufficient funds to increase the gross enrollment ratio in our higher education institutions. This makes the students affordable for higher education, especially those students who are away from higher education due to poverty. Lack of quality; is another major problem, which is facing the higher education system in India. Ensuring quality in higher education is the foremost challenge being faced in India today. Though the government is persistently focusing on the quality of education, a large number of colleges and universities are unable to meet the minimum requirements laid down by the UGC due to a lack of sufficient funds. The expenditure incurred on education only 3.1% (Economic Survey, 2019-20) of GDP as against 6% recommended by the Kothari Commission in 1964. In the case of research and development, it is only 0.6% of GDP, but it is 2.79% and 2.15% for U.S.A and China, respectively (World Bank, 2018). Even after the completion of six decades, we are unable to implement the recommendations of the Kothari Commission. Quality in higher education also attracts foreign students. 47,427 foreign students enrolled from 164 different countries across the globe, out of which 63.7% are from neighboring countries, *i.e.*, Nepal, having 26.88% of the total, followed by Afghanistan (9.8%), Bangladesh (4.38%), Sudan (4.02%), Bhutan constitutes (3.82%) and Nigeria (3.4%). India seeks to attract 2 Lakh foreign students, nearly four times the current number. This is possible only through increasing expenditure on education to provide all sorts of infrastructural facilities and efficient faculty. Lack of infrastructure facilities; is also one of the major problems and it has become a big challenge to the higher education system in India, about 77.8% colleges are privately managed and most of them are functioning in apartments, which have no playground, laboratories and library facilities. Some government colleges/institutes also suffer from poor physical infrastructure facilities. This demonstrates the backwardness of the higher education system in India. Hence the governments, both central and state level, should concentrate on these areas to strengthen educational institutions in India. Political Interference is certainly the most important reason for poor outcomes in the education sector in India. Most of the educational institutions are owned by political leaders, who are playing key roles in governing bodies of the universities and they make education a profitable business. This results in the mushrooming of private educational institutions and poor outcomes. Scarcity of faculty; is another problem in HEIs in India. The inability of the state educational system in attracting and retaining well qualified teachers has become a challenge to quality education for many years. Large numbers of NET/PhD qualified candidates are unemployed even though there are a lot of vacancies in higher educational institutions; then, these deserving candidates are applying for other jobs for their livelihood and take underemployment, which is the biggest blow to the higher education system. When it comes to NAAC accreditation, only 606 universities and 12709 colleges were accredited, which is 61% and 31.8%, respectively and which is shown in Figs. (**3** and **4**). Among these accredited, only 34.15% of the universities and 13.32% of the colleges were found to be of quality to be ranked at 'A' level", as per the data provided by the NAAC as of January 2020. The statistics show the quality of higher education is very poor and alarming. Hence more attention has to be given to the quality enhancement of HE institutions both at the university and college level in India.

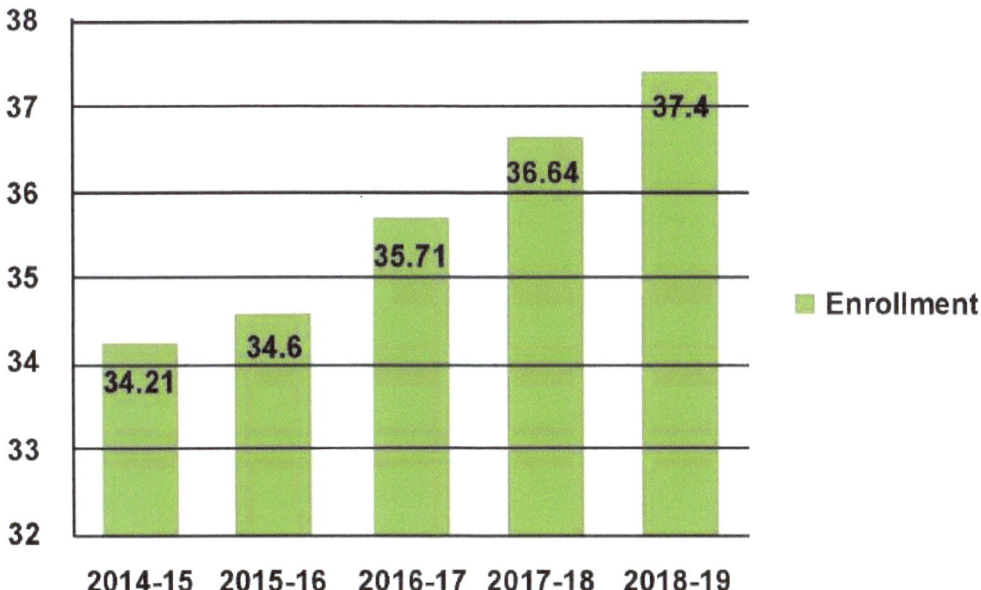

Fig. (3). Enrollment in various years.

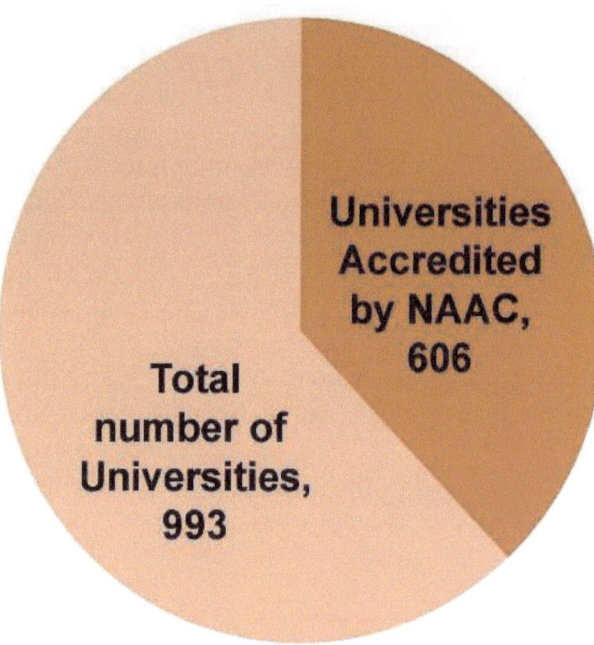

Fig. (4). Universities accredited.

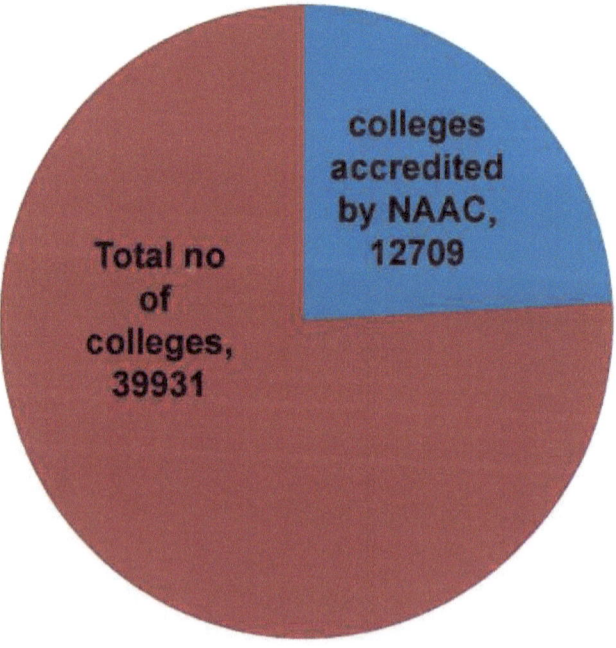

Fig. (5). Colleges accredited.

Inadequate focus on research; There is an inadequate focus on research in higher education institutions, especially in social sciences and insufficient resources, infrastructure facilities, as well as limited numbers of quality faculty to advise research scholars. India has a few eminent scholars, whose writings are cited by eminent authors of the rest of the world. Most of the research scholars are without fellowships or not getting their fellowships on time, which directly or indirectly affects their research, which further de-motivates their research. Moreover, Indian Higher education institutions are poorly connected to research centers and the shortage of teaching faculty, an increasing number of affiliated colleges and students, the burden of administrative functions have significantly increased due to shortage of non-teaching staff and this results low focus on academics and research.

PROSPECTS OF HIGHER EDUCATION

India is the 2nd largest populated country having a more young population aged between 18-23 years, and it is in the middle of the demographic dividend with a surge in younger and working age population, estimated to become the world's largest by 2030. This massive size of the market offers huge opportunities for the development of the higher education sector in India. India now possesses 39,931 colleges and 993 universities, which has been quite a significant growth during the last three decades. The total enrollment increased to 37.40 million in 2018-19, which makes India one of the largest educational systems in the world. Unfortunately, the existing educational infrastructure facilities of India are inadequate to handle such huge volumes of market. The current government expenditure in the educational sector is too insufficient to meet the growing requirements of the younger population. Therefore, the higher education sector has now been identified as one of the potential areas for private and foreign investments.

Irrespective of various problems and challenges, the Indian higher education system is growing very rapidly during the last three decades. With the help of modern learning tools, it is very easy to overcome these problems and bring a paradigm shift in the country's higher education sector in India. With such a vibrant country with a huge population properly educated, the possibilities are endless. If knowledge is imparted using advanced digital teaching and learning tools and society is made aware of, where we are currently lagging behind, our country can easily emerge as one of the most developed nations in the world (Younis A.S, 2017). At this moment, the modern learning tools like digital education, virtual learning, internships and online learning have created an opportunity to become India as an educational hub. By attracting foreign investments in education, we can create good infrastructure and attract high quality faculty, which will further open the gates for collaboration with international institutions. Finally all these measures help in preventing brain drain from India.

SUGGESTIONS TO IMPROVE THE QUALITY OF HIGHER EDUCATION

It is suggested to develop innovative, transforming multidisciplinary approaches to meet the needs of the growing global competitiveness. It is suggested that collaborations with industries are to be increased for the development of curriculum, organizing expert lectures, internships, live projects, career counseling and placements. Political intervention should be strictly avoided by the education system. It is also suggested to make the strict implementation of norms of MHRD/UGC in all private institutions. It is suggested that, strengthening of the alumni, make use of its contributions, placements, mentorship, scholarship and Career Guidance, *etc*. Government should strengthen the Bio-metric attendance system, (GPS enabled Bio-metric system) and expand it to private institutions while making it mandatory. It is also suggested that the government should also implement and increase merit based student scholarship to improve the quality of education and outcomes. Government should concentrate on regular mode appointments of faculty and also encourage, create an environment to pursue research through FIP. It is suggested to implement the recommendation of Kothari Commission *i.e.* expenditure on education should be increased to 6% of GDP. Government must promote collaboration between Indian higher educational institutes with top International institutes and also generate linkage between national research laboratories and research centers of top institutions for better quality and collaborative research.

The growth of higher education institutions plays an important role in the development of any country. This chapter gives a brief outlook of these institutions on the present growth status. The quality of physical infrastructure and faculty is a key point for these institutions to find a place in world ranking. It discusses the practical problems and opportunities and suggested measures to improve the quality of these institutions. The data analysis and discussions of the chapter are useful for the higher education institutions in analyzing their current situation, formulating their policies to improve the quality of the institutions and secure a better place in India and world rankings.

CONCLUSION

Higher education plays an important role in economic development. Soon after independence, the Government of India established UGC and later MHRD to improve the quality of higher education in India. The number of universities and colleges has grown significantly during the last three decades and this quantity of higher education institutions makes no sense without the quality. Hence it is time to focus on problems that hamper the development of the quality of higher education in India. Given this background, we studied and identified some problems and challenges of higher education, like poor quality of education & research, lack of infrastructure facilities, shortage of faculty, political interference, *etc.* We also studied the prospects of higher education and made some suggestions to improve quality. Here we conclude that infrastructure facilities as well as the quality of faculty will contribute to better outcomes in higher education. Hence in order to meet the challenges of the higher education system today, the government should spend sufficient financial resources on education and strictly implement Government/UGC norms in all institutions, including privately owned/managed to achieve better outcomes.

CONSENT FOR PUBLICATION

Not applicable.

CONFLICT OF INTEREST

The author declares no conflict of interest, financial or otherwise.

ACKNOWLEDGEMENTS

Declared none.

REFERENCES

AISHE. (2010-11). Ministry of human resource development, government of India, New Delhi. https://www.education.gov.in/sites/upload_files/mhrd/files/statistics/AISHE201011.pdf

AISHE. (2018). Ministry of Human Resource Development, Government of India, New Delhi. https://aishe.gov.in/aishe/viewDocument.action;jsessionid=BD8F531947B30B54A6C6DEA0ABF32D2B.n1?documentId=262

Economic Survey (2019-20), volume -2:Government of India, Ministry of Finance Department of Economic Affairs Economic Division. North Block. New Delhi: *110001*, 275. https://www.indiabudget.gov.in/budget2020-21/economicsurvey/doc/echapter_vol2.pdf

Higher Education, Policy and Development in Asia. (2017). International comparison: gross enrollment ratio. https://edblogs.columbia.edu/inafu6653-001-2017-1/2017/02/08/international-comparison-gross-enrolment-ratio/

Sharma, S., Sharma, P. (2015). Indian higher education system: challenges and suggestions. *Electronic J Inclusive Education,* *3*(4). https://corescholar.libraries.wright.edu/cgi/viewcontent.cgi?article= 1179&context=ejie

World bank open data base.

Younis, A.S. (2017). Higher education in India, challenges and opportunities. *J. Educ Pract, 8*(1), 39-42. https://files.eric.ed.gov/fulltext/EJ1131773.pdf

CHAPTER 12

Performance of Higher Education in India

K. Chakrapati[1,*]

[1] Department of Economics, Goverment Degree College Pathapatnam, Srikakulam, Dr. B.R. Ambedkar University, Srikakulam, India

Abstract: Education is the most powerful weapon to change the social, economic, and cultural, backwardness. Particularly higher education with research and development drives the country towards a good economic position in all aspects. India occupies the second position regarding the highest populated countries in the world. At the same time, India also enjoys the advantage of demographic dividend occupying the top place with respect to the youth population. Keeping pace with the global developments, if effective measures are implemented in the field of education, India's manpower can be transformed into quality human resources. As a developing country, India has been prioritizing universalization of education, resulting in its horizontal growth. Now India should also focus on vertical growth with skill-oriented education especially at higher levels. India is the second-highest population country but first place in the younger (youth) generation. This paper mainly focuses on the overall performance of the higher education system in India. It also identifies required solutions and plans to be used for the improvement of quality in higher education in India.

Keywords: Distance Education, Gross Enrollment Ratio, Empower, Enrollment, Higher Education, Higher Education System, Learning Strategies, Methodology, Opportunities, Pedagogical Issues, Primary Education, Privatization, Professional, Self Sustainability, Skill development, Technical Education, Vocational.

INTRODUCTION

Higher education system includes academic institutions that include universities, colleges and vocational institutions. These institutions prepare professionals for all sectors of the economy. In a knowledgeable society, these institutions are enablers of research, innovation and entrepreneurship. They help address the problems in a society and nations and prepare individuals for their life and career. Thus they play an important role in shaping our future. Higher education provides opportunities to the people to reflect on critical issues faced by humanity in social, cultural, economic fields. Higher education provides specialized knowledge and

---

[*] **Corresponding author K. Chakrapati:** Department of Economics, Goverment Degree College Pathapatnam, Srikakulam, Dr. B.R. Ambedkar University, Srikakulam, India; Tel: 8179820908; E-mail: chakrapatik@gmail.com

Sankara Narayana Rao Gedala and P.L. Saranya (Eds)
All rights reserved-© 2021 Bentham Science Publishers

skilled manpower for national development. India will have the world's largest set of young people. The increasing youth population can be a great asset if skill oriented education is provided. India can no longer continue with the model of universal education; rather it requires more investment in human resources to make them productive by adding field-based experience to traditional disciplines of natural sciences, commerce, humanities and social sciences to enhance knowledge with concerned skills and attitudes.

ISSUES WITH HIGHER EDUCATION IN INDIA

To compete in a globalized economy India needs highly skilled professionals. The present education system is producing graduates in great numbers but their quality is not so encouraging. Most of the reports (Power K,B., 2002) said that higher education institutes are not at satisfactory levels in terms of access, equity and equality. Government should give priority to education sector and focus on its development to get the emerging opportunities and handle the challenges of the 21st century. The following are the sum of issues with higher education in India.

Teaching Quality

It may be true that well-qualified, experienced and enthusiastic teachers are found in the prestigious institutes like IITs, IIMs and central universities but in the state universities the required things are political influence and recommendation. There is no correct monetary policy on teaching-learning financing: Out of the total budget allocated to higher education, 65% of the funds is going to central universities and the remaining 35% only, is being spent on nearly 400 state universities. We are not able to find sufficient funds to research and development.

Privatization

After 1990's education was also commercialized and it has been on the path of privatization. Most of the private educational institutions are getting profit of crores of rupees, by starting professional courses. The trend of more cost, more the benefit is going on. These private institutions are out of reach to the students of middle class and lower class families. It leads to inequality and unrest in the society.

Quota System

Reservations in the teaching field sometimes may not give expected standards in education. Students scoring minimum of marks may get a seat or a post instead of a merit student. So there will be doubts about how he/she can justify the post and maintain the standard in giving a better future in the education field.

Political Factors

Involvement of politicians in higher education diversified the education system and as a result, it became a profitable business. Sometimes educational institutes are started for getting tax exemption and fee reimbursement benefits.

Moral Issues

Education means knowledge, skill and character building. Ethics and moral values should be developed besides giving professional knowledge. At present, higher education may help in acquiring skills and earning money, but, due to lack of moral values, higher educators themselves are indulging in anti-social activities. Parents and corporate colleges concentrate on marks and ranks, and give priority to science subjects, neglecting languages, where we can find ethics and values.

Challenges in Higher Education

Though higher education in India has a long history, now it is facing many difficulties and troubles. The main problem in Indian higher education institutions is the shortage of faculties. As per the recent studies, 35% of the faculty positions are vacant. Most of the faculties lack quality teaching, research and training. In addition to this, some additional issues are also there. The standing committee of human resource development chaired by Dr. Satyanarayana Jathiya submitted its report on 'Issues and challenges of higher education in India' on February 18th, 2017.

The key observations and recommendations of the committee are as follows:

Shortage of Resources

As per the committee report, state universities and affiliated colleges under the universities together receive only 35% of the funds given by UGC, where the majority of students study. UGC concentrates more on central universities and 65% of funds are allotted to them. The committee advised state universities to mobilize funds from alumni, endowment, industries *etc*.

Vacancies in Teaching

According to the committee, 35% of the posts are vacant even in central universities. As far as state universities are concerned, 80% of the teaching staff work on a contract basis or as guest faculty.

Accountability and Performance of Teachers

Except for passing percentages, there is no particular feedback about a teacher. In addition to passing percentages, content development, and the use of ICT by the teacher and marks of the students, should be taken into account. Orientation and refresher training should be given to teachers time to time.

LACK OF EMPLOYABLE SKILLS

The committee observed lack of skills in students of technical education especially in engineering and management. It recommended to introduce courses promoting employment (Mishra Sharda, 2006). Some strategies in this regard include, industrial challenge open forum, industry institute student training support, long term industry placement scheme and industrial finishing schools (Naveen Chahal, 2015). Accreditation of institutions: A national board of accreditation should act as a catalyst towards quality enhancement and quality assurance of institutions.

THE MOST COMMON CHALLENGES

The following are some common problems faced by the higher education sector in India. The curricula and syllabus are old and outdated. There is no sufficient staff in higher educational institutions in India. There is not serious focus on skill development programmes. Teaching methods and evaluation systems are not advanced. Students have few opportunities to develop skills like analytical reasoning, problem-solving, critical thinking and collaborative working. Because of not giving importance to values in pedagogy, value-based qualitative education is not being followed strictly. Only teaching is given priority and there is a lack of emphasis on research. Prestigious academic institutions like IITs, IIMs, AIIMS and IISc have less than 1% of the total students only. Fees in those institutions are also not affordable by students of weaker sections. We do not find our institutions or universities in the list of top 100 in the world. The situation results in low employability opportunities for Indian graduates. The disparity in economic growth and unequal access to opportunities adversely affect the enrollment trends in higher education. In India, expenditure on higher education and research is low. The Indian education system is more focused on theoretical knowledge rather than practical knowledge. As per the NAAC report, 68% of the universities and 90% of the colleges are of poor quality, because of insufficient regular teaching staff and the practice of only traditional methods of teaching. There is no thrust to use updated technology and audiovisual aids in teaching. In India, still being a developing country, public sector institutions suffer from a lack of physical facilities and infrastructure. In the globalized economy, our education skills must be up to the levels of global expectations. Otherwise, there will be no way to develop and compete other nations. Some of the universities and higher education institutions are knowingly or unknowingly involved in politics. Students forget their own objectives and begin to develop their careers in politics.

SUGGESTIONS FOR IMPROVING THE QUALITY OF HIGHER EDUCATION

Some valuable suggestions have been given by employees and authorities for the improvement of quality in higher education. We should enhance our competence up to global competitive levels. Higher educational institutes need to improve quality and reputation. The higher education institutes must collaborate with top international institutes, and research laboratories. We should focus on excellence so that they will get jobs after completion of studies. Methods of teaching have to be appropriate to the needs of learners. Modern methods like virtual classroom-teaching should be followed. Video lessons by efficient teachers should be made available on the internet for the benefit of backward rural students (Mukesh Chahal, 2015). Continuous assessment of learning must be implemented for the constant improvement of students. As per the recommendations of the National Knowledge Commission 2005, a number of universities have been established to increase gross enrollment. But still they are suffering from a lack of infrastructure and regular based-teaching faculty. The government should concentrate on recruiting sufficient staff and promoting mutual co-operation among the higher education institutes of the country. Educational tours should be encouraged so that students get knowledge about different cultures and lifestyles in different regions.

The second and third-grade government institutes are not getting sufficient public funds to upgrade their IT infrastructure, which is crucial to attracting cross-country students. This is a prerequisite for achieving a good rank in the ranking framework. Policymakers need to think about this aspect.

CONCLUSION

Since independence, we have been giving priority to the universalization of education as a basic need to the growing population. Even after the completion of 12 five-year plans, ¼th of the population remain illiterates. Since the nineties we have focused on technical, vocational and, professional courses for qualitative human resources. The government allotted a major part of the education budget to prioritized institutions like IITs, IIMs, AIIMS and made the students somewhat competitive globally supplying quality human workforce to multinational companies. Institutions should adopt changing curricula and teaching methods to meet the changing demand of modern society. The policymakers and monitoring and regulating bodies must identify the hurdles and make quick decisions to drive our educational system forward. Only then, our country would become one of the developed countries in the world.

CONSENT FOR PUBLICATION

Not applicable.

CONFLICT OF INTEREST

The author declares no conflict of interest, financial or otherwise.

ACKNOWLEDGEMENTS

Declared none.

REFERENCES

Mishra, S. (2006). *UGC and Higher Education System in India.* Book Enclare, Jaipur. https://www.abebooks.com/servlet/SearchResults?ltrec=t&isbn=9788181521484&bi=

Mukesh, C. (2015). Higher education in India, emerging issues, challenges and suggestions. *Int J Business Quantative Economic and Applied Management Research,* 1(11). http://ijbemr.com/wp-content/uploads/2015/05/Higher_Education_in_India_Emerging_Issues_Challenges_and_Suggestions.pdf

Naveen, C., Hafizullah, D. (2015). Higher education sector in India: challenges of sustainability. *International J Manag Res & Review,* 5(3), 159. google scholar

Power, K.B. (2002). Indian higher education: a conglomerate of concept, fats, and, practices. New Delhi: Concept publication company. https://www.conceptpub.com/servlet/Detail?bookno=00000686

CHAPTER 13

Higher Education In India - Issues and Challenges

Godavari Venkata Murali Mohan[1,*]

[1] *Department of Telugu, Government College for Women Autonomous Srikakulam, Dr. B.R. Ambedkar University, Srikakulam, India*

Abstract: The vision and aims of higher education in India are grand- to tap the inviolate demographic resources of the country and equip them with enough opportunities so as to ensure nation-building and development. Ever since the country's independence, all the policies and programs aimed at the redemption of higher education of India have been aiming at this particular issue. This sector has always provided innumerable opportunities for national development but is also marred with a lot of challenges and practical difficulties that delay the progress. Education is not only a tool for social progress, but also the means to achieve political and economic freedom. Though there are a plethora of policies which envisage a proper structure and progress for higher development, inadequate stress on the quality of education has been one of the biggest issues concerning the sector. This research paper discusses the various challenges and issues faced by higher education in India and the way ahead.

Keywords: Accessibility, AICTE, Challenges, Collaboration, Higher education, Human development, Employability, Empowerment, Enrollment, Enrollment of students, Politicization, Privatization, Right to education, Regulatory bodies, Research and development, Udaan, UGC, Unemployment.

INTRODUCTION

India is the second most populous country in the world and the current demographic dividend India possesses makes us one of the youngest countries in the world. We have one of the largest schooling systems, and the number of schools, colleges and universities will only exemplify the fact that the education sector in India is predominant and vast with many focal points. The right to education act passed by the Indian parliament and the fundamental right that guarantees basic and free education have made the concept of education a much bigger force to reckon within the Indian context. The state and central governments have been investing huge amounts in all ways to improve functional

---

[*] **Corresponding author Godavari Venkata Murali Mohan:** Department of Economics, Govt. Degree College Pathapatnam, Srikakulam, Dr. B.R. Ambedkar University, Srikakulam, India; Tel: 9493907898;
E-mail: murali51165@gmail.com

Sankara Narayana Rao Gedala and P.L. Saranya (Eds)
All rights reserved-© 2021 Bentham Science Publishers

and nominal literacy across all the spectra. In such a revolutionary juncture, it is important to revisit the state of higher education in our country, steps taken by the government since independence to reform higher education, the challenges that are lurking underneath the implementation of those policies, and the way ahead.

HIGHER EDUCATION IN INDIA SINCE INDEPENDENCE

As higher education systems grow and diversify, society is increasingly concerned regarding the quality of programs, public assessments and international rankings of higher education institutions. However, these comparisons tend to overemphasize research, using research performance as a yardstick of institutional value. If these processes fail to address the quality of teaching, it is in part because measuring teaching quality is challenging (Henard, 2008). India has always been the land of the gurus and the sages who imparted immense knowledge in all sciences and arts. The earliest texts in medicine, arts, sciences and technology, astrology and astronomy belonged to the Indian scholars. India was the seat of learning with many universities like Taxila, Nalanda, Vikramshila and others where many scholars not only from within the country but also from all sections of the world came and studied. The British rule reduced the impact of the higher education system for a bit. Since independence, the central government and state governments have immensely tried to reform the higher education sector by founding and installing various universities dedicated to higher education. Some of the most important ones are the Indian Institutes of Technology. The level of government involvement has been increasing over the years, with many things, the most notable of them being the founding of the University Grants Commission (UGC). It has been at the forefront as a focal point of all the university education in the country. Over the years, the UGC has brought a lot of quality to the way higher education is implemented in the country through a certain set of standards for all universities and institutions. Even with the involvement of the university grants commission, many colleges and universities are still not following the norms put forth by the highest institution for excellence in higher education.

Along with the UGC, there is a plethora of research councils and regulatory bodies that have been constituted by the government of India over the course of time. They are as follows (Sharma & Sharma, 2015): The All India Council of Technical Education (AICTE) set up to oversee the technical education scenario in our country; Council of Architecture (COA) and regulatory bodies such as the Indian Council of Medical Research (ICMR), the Indian Council of Historical Research (ICHR), the National Council of Rural Institute (NCRI), and Indian Council of Philosophical Research (ICPR).

One of the biggest changes that occurred in the Indian higher education after independence in general and after the economic reforms in particular, is the introduction of private players into the higher education. Though education has to be one of the state's responsibilities towards the people, the mushrooming of private institutions of learning at all levels of primary, secondary and higher, has drastically impacted the inclusion of more students into the higher education. These institutions run mainly for monetary benefits, completely disregarding the fact that education has to be one of the areas without any biases and reservations. This brings out a major ripple effect making it difficult for the poor and unprivileged people to attain admissions in those institutions. Some of the major issues dealing with privatization and its effects are as follows (Gogoi, 2019): Education is being run as a business in private institutions rather than a tool for development and empowerment. Thus, the very moral responsibility of the state to make sure each and every citizen is entitled to free and accessible education is being nullified. This will stymie critical thinking in individuals since education has become a business. The next important thing is accessibility. India after independence, during its early years, aimed at having a socialistic pattern of society, where each and every citizen of the society is entitled to have equal access to all the national resources. Privatization disrupts that philosophy. Education is perceived as a basic human right. In order to have equal opportunities in all walks of life, all citizens must have equal access to higher education. Though the right to education act was constituted in 2009, there has been little to no progress in this arena. The concept of the right to education is completely antithetical to privatization. Organizations that are run with profit motives cannot dedicate their moral values towards ensuring universal access of education to everyone.

CHALLENGES

However, these exercises are not without challenges and higher education in the country is faced with these as follows (Sheikh, 2017); Enrollment of students: it is extremely low, which is not even compared to the other developed countries. Even if the higher number of enrollment of students is witnessed, there is no essential infrastructure of the universities to impart quality education. The equity of the gross enrollment ratio is absent. The gross enrollment ratio of female students is deplorable and is unevenly distributed. Some states have a higher rate of enrollment while others cannot boast much. Quality of education: the most important thing that is essential for the successful running of higher education in India is a good quality of education. No matter how many institutes are established, if there is no emphasis on the quality of education, it does not meet the minimum requirements to make a mark in the world. Infrastructure: this is one of the major problems plaguing higher education. Irregular and inadequate spending by government on higher education and its infrastructure in universities is leading to poor infrastructure of colleges and universities. That, in turn, is reducing the quality of higher education. Politicization of education and institutions is also one of the major issues plaguing the sector. Many of the institutions are run by political leaders lacking in basic norms. Research and innovation: no importance to jobs and having degrees without any know-how the way research and innovation are done, has led to the colleges functioning like factories producing mass robots. Finally, there is no political will to radicalize and revolutionize higher education for addressing real issues like poverty and unemployment. Due to the irregular and incomplete policies of the government, unemployment has been skyrocketing.

OPPORTUNITIES AHEAD

Amidst the uneven challenges faced by higher education, there exist many opportunities which can also be made use of if the government and institutions function perfectly. The unique demographic dividend the country enjoys can actually be used to increase the riches and make India a more developed country with a higher standard of living. If enough research and development are allocated to the higher education sector, the government can keep a check on unemployment, which in turn can eradicate poverty and social ills. Programs like "Udaan" need better encouragement and implementation to enrich the poor and unprivileged with basic resources and necessities of life, such as education. It has to be made more competitive and a transformation is needed to make a change. Through more relevance and competitiveness in the higher education sector, it can be made more world-class and can cater to the needs of more people. Also, the government must encourage collaborations between organizations and small institutions to increase the quality of education imparted by smaller institutions. Through overseeing smaller organizations, the big universities will get a chance to lend their curriculum to the colleges, and that in turn can improve the quality of education.

Some important things the education sector in India must impart and avoid are undue affiliation with politicians and politics of all kind. Due to excessive political influence, the education sector in India is becoming politicized and missing the real agenda. India is a country where a large section of the population still does not have access to basic education and empowerment. In order to make it happen, it is important that top priority is given to get the basics right not letting the external factors impede progress. By concentrating more on infrastructure, investing more in research and development, and creating more avenues for higher education, India can successfully envision a great future for higher education and graduates, which will spike the growth and development of the country. As higher education is the most important phase in any student's life, it has to be given the importance it demands.

India ranks very low in terms of the quality of the research work that is produced by research organizations. It is important to note that though there is a lot of funding that goes into higher education and research, it needs to be increased to cater to the huge demographic dividend that India has. The workforce needs knowledge and training to be adequately imparted to them through efficient methods in order to ensure both economic growth and human development. If that does not happen, India will continue to have economic growth but will stand behind in terms of human development indices. Plans need to be made to increase programs that contribute to the high employability of graduates that come out of colleges every year. There has to be a sufficient number of collaborations with the industry and educational institutions to make the quality of education better. A lot needs to be learned from the West, where human development and the development in higher education are directly proportional to each other. There is a huge demand for higher education in India with the rising youth population and the number of students that are graduating every year. The supply and the demand need to be matched.

After independence, the higher education scenario in India has undergone a tectonic shift. With the ever-increasing population and the rising rate of youth for becoming entitled to the higher education, it becomes absolutely essential for the governments to create a progressive space for the development of higher education in India. Though a number of challenges keep lurking around the corner, there is always immense scope for improvement in this arena. In this chapter, the challenges that confront the higher education system in India and the way ahead for growth in the sector are discussed.

The various governing bodies, research councils, and regulatory institutions of higher education are mentioned. The issues and challenges the system faces due to the inherent changes that were brought forth in higher education, such as privatization, are discussed in detail. Along with that, the other challenges the sector faces and the opportunities that lie in the road to development are described.

CONCLUSION

In the 21st century, education is the most important tool to weed out poverty, gain employment and increase the standard of living for any citizen. It is due to the lack of a strong education background of the workforce that countries like India are still not embracing the path of development on a sustainable basis. For development and growth that lead to an increased standard of life, emphasis on higher education as part of government policy and planning is a must. Through transparent and accountable methods, a national strategy regarding higher education should be endeavored to achieve success in this sector.

CONSENT FOR PUBLICATION

Not applicable.

CONFLICT OF INTEREST

The author declares no conflict of interest, financial or otherwise.

ACKNOWLEDGEMENTS

Declared none.

REFERENCES

Gogoi, P.P. (2019). Privatization of education in india is anti-poor and anti-people. https://www.youthkiawaaz.com/2019/01/why-privatization-of-education-is-anti-poor-and-anti-people/

Henard, F., Leprince-Ringuet, S. (2008). The path to quality teaching in higher education. París: OCDE. https://www.oecd.org/education/imhe/44150246.pdf

Sharma, S., Sharma, P. (2015). Indian higher education system: challenges and suggestions. *Electron. J. Incl. Educ., 3*(4), 6. https://corescholar.libraries.wright.edu/cgi/viewcontent.cgi?article=1179&context=ejie

Sheikh, Y.A. (2017). Higher education in India: Challenges and opportunities. *J. Educ. Pract., 8*(1), 39-42. https://eric.ed.gov/?id=EJ1131773

CHAPTER 14

Characteristics of Teaching and Learning - A Study on Challenges

A. Ramarao[1,*] and Karri Rama Rao[2]

[1] Department of Economics, Goverment Degree College, Tekkali, Dr. B.R. Ambedkar University Srikakulam, Tekkali, Srikakulam Dist, Andhra Pradesh, India

[2] Department of Zoology, Goverment Degree College, Tekkali, Srikakulam Dt. Dr. B.R. Ambedkar University, Srikakulam, Andhra Pradesh, India

Abstract: A great deal has been spoken and debated about the characteristics of effective teaching and learning at college or universities. Much more focus has been paid to attributes of a good teacher than to the leaner today. Though there are many conferences and seminars deliberating on this important issue which affected thousands of learners across the globe in terms of diversity, need and adequacy, yet it is still less. Many approaches like cooperative learning, self directed learning, student centric learning and teacher's style have to be worked upon in depth to offer the advantage to the learner. It is undoubtedly a complicated matter, there is no indication of one best way to demand holistic understanding of the context and the learner's needs and challenges.

Keywords: Assignment, Co-operative learning, Diversity of learners, Effective teaching, Inspiration, Self directed learning, Syllabus, Teaching and Learning, Teaching strategies, Teaching techniques.

INTRODUCTION

Learning and teaching should not stand on opposite banks and just watch the river flow by; instead, they should embark together on a Journey down the water. The Italian early childhood education specialist was right in his perspective of viewing teaching and learning as two sides of the same coin. Simple as it seems, quite paradoxical though it is, teaching and learning have to be corrected as the same point of time for us educationists or teachers to conclude that learning has happened in our everyday arena called the classroom. But many times we are under the misconception that the teacher teaches and the learner learns, which is an inaccuracy in thought, where one approach fits all. A carefully planned lesson

---

* **Corresponding author A. Ramarao:** Department of Economics, Goverment Degree College, Tekkali, Dr. B.R. Ambedkar University Srikakulam, Tekkali, Srikakulam Dist, Andhra Pradesh, India; Tel: 7780668430; E-mail: ramarao.ampolu@gmail.com

Sankara Narayana Rao Gedala and P.L. Saranya (Eds)
All rights reserved-© 2021 Bentham Science Publishers

might inspire one student to craft an amazing story, committed to improve his/her grades and go on to college to become a journalist. The same lesson might leave another child confused and discouraged. Effective teaching requires flexibility and creativity. We teachers often find these questions perplexing with no satisfactory answers. What made us feel so good because of the thought that we delivered well in the classroom in one day. The same may backfire on another day with the same group. Is it because we take learners for granted or is it that we have failed to match our teaching strategies with the context and our learners' needs. It is imperative to reflect on these questions on an everyday basis. We must constantly monitor and adjust our teaching techniques. What we don't have to do is reinvent the wheel for every lesson (Ramsden, 1992, Senge, 1990).

OBSERVATIONS

Characteristics of Teaching and Learning

1. A Complex Social Process: Teaching is a complex social phenomenon, it is greatly influenced by social factors.

2. Art as Well as Science: Teaching is both art and science. To be sure, teaching-like the practice of medicine; is very much an art which is to say, calls for exercise of talent and creativity. Like medicine, it is also a science, for it involves a repertoire of techniques, procedures and skills that can be systematically studied and described and improved. Like a great doctor, a good teacher adds creativity and inspiration to the basic repertoire.

3. A Professional Activity: Teaching is a professional activity involving the teacher and the student, resulting in the development of the student.

4. Output Emanating from the Teacher: Teaching is what the teacher does with his student that causes the latter to learn something and it is purely an outcome of the teacher's efforts.

5. Amenable to Scientific Observation and Analysis: What is going on in teaching can be observed, analyzed and assessed through the teacher's behaviour pupil-teacher interactions and the changes brought in the behavior of the pupils.

6. An Interactive Process: Teaching is an interactive process carried out for the attainment of the specific purpose and objectives.

7. Learning is a process and not a product.

8. Learning is the shaping of beliefs, knowledge and behavior of the learner.

9. Learning is a process that brings relatively permanent changes in the behavior of the learner through experience or practice.

10. A specialized task comprising different teaching skills: Teaching is a specialized task and may be taken as a set of component skills for the realization of a specified set of instructional objectives as observed by Jangira and Ajit Singh, (1982), Mangal Umamangal, (2016).

Challenges of Teaching and Learning components that can be discussed are endless, yet it is worth exploring some of them for effective teaching learning in a classroom. Cooperative learning techniques allow every student in the class to participate much of the time, but, as many students are involved in this activity, they should be organized in such a way that it is productive but not chaotic.

RESULTS AND DISCUSSION

Higher order thinking offers its own interpretations of topics to solve problems. Learning interpersonal skills is increasingly recognized as an important life skill, both for productive work on the job, for happy family life, and for participation in a democratic society. They are promoting interpersonal and inter-group understanding. Creating an interesting atmosphere involves, knowing what students understand and then knowing connections between what is known and what is new. One probable equation for instilling motivation for learning through excitement is quality. Students feel more attached to the school and the class leading to better attendance and higher retention rates. Independence, control and active engagement are essential things. As good teachers, we must create innovative and customized learning tasks appropriate to the student's level of understanding. Researchers also recognize the uniqueness of individual learners and avoid the temptation to impose "mass production" standards that treat all learners as if they belonged to the herd. Encouraging self-directed learning is another important aspect. "No matter how good teaching may be each student must take responsibility for his own education." (Morrow and Others, 1993). A situated learning approach is that in which teachers bring real-life problems into the classroom for learners to work on. They advise against 'Sugar –coating', the rationale is that, if the tasks are meaningful, learners will work on them willingly. Every effective teacher must instill confidence in the learner to bring about a considerable change in the system or environment for one's own and societal benefit. This concept is most often referred to as action research. Unless this critical thinking path is nurtured the next generation learners will become people with no solid values. If a student cannot wonder at the marvels of nature and everyday phenomena around them, the seed of curiosity which is the basis for research, will never be sown in the learners' minds. We must not forget that it was only the falling apple which made Issac Newton curiously wonder and discover the Law of Gravitation (Corno, 1992). One who looks back with appreciation to the brilliant teacher, but with gratitude to those who touched our human feelings. The curriculum is so much necessary warm material, but warmth is a vital element for the growing plant and for the soul of the child. In the rat race for outstanding grade and comparative assessment indicators coupled with the 'job factor', teachers many a time forget to be humane and treat their students with love and consideration. On one hand it is an unfinished syllabus and on the other hand, it is their own egoistic feeling and self-overrating which pushes them up the wall to make their learners only doers and not 'thinkers'. Teachers must lead through their exemplary behaviour in acquiring knowledge, handling students, maintaining cordial relationships with others and administrative responsibilities. If students find the gap between teaching and practice, it is impossible to convert them into willing learners as their minds are preoccupied with questioning the credibility of their teachers (Silverman, 1978).

CONCLUSION

Effective teaching refuses to take its effect on students for granted and it sees the relation between teaching and learning as problematic, uncertain and relative. Good teaching is open to change, and it involves constant trying to find out what the effects of instruction are on learning and modifying the instruction in the light of the evidence collected. The two elements teaching and learning have to be ever evolving and changing paradigms, parameters and possibilities. Until then, they continue to remain paradoxical. True learning is a kind of natural food for the mind and never taught.

Creating a better environment for teaching learning improves the chances of obtaining a good rank in ranking framework methodologies.

CONSENT FOR PUBLICATION

Not applicable.

CONFLICT OF INTEREST

The author declares no conflict of interest, financial or otherwise.

ACKNOWLEDGEMENTS

The authors thank Commissioner of Collegiate Education and Principal, Govt. Degree College, Tekkali, Srikakulam Dt. Andhra Pradesh for their constant encouragement during the study periods.

REFERENCES

Corno, L. (1992). Encouraging students to take responsibilities for Learning and Performance. *The Elementary School Journal.*
[http://dx.doi.org/10.1086/461713]

Jangira, N.K., Ajit, Singh (1983). Core teaching skills: the micro-teaching approach. New Delhi: NCERT. https://www.worldcat.org/title/core-teaching-skills-the-microteaching-approach-handbook-for-secondary-teacher-education/oclc/70329029

Mangal Umamangal, S.K. (2016). Essential of educational technology, PHI. https://www.amazon.in/Essentials-Educational-Technology-S-K-Mangal-Mangal-ebook/dp/B00K7YG1NE

Morrow, L.M. (1993). Promoting independent reading and writing through self-directed literacy activities in a collaborative setting. Reading Research Report No.2. https://files.eric.ed.gov/fulltext/ED356455.pdf

Ramsden, P., Donald, Bligh (1992). Learning to teach in higher education. *J. Studies in Education,* New York.*18*(1), 290.
[http://dx.doi.org/10.1080/03075079312331382498]

Silverman, R.E. (1978). *Psychology: Study Guide and Workbook.* (3rd ed.). Englewood Cliffs, N.J.: Prentice Hall. https://www.abebooks.com/servlet/BookDetailsPL?bi=30287847323

Senge, P.M. (1990). The Fifth Discipline; The Art and Practice of the Learning Organization. (pp. 1-412). New York: Doubleday Currency. http://kmcenter.rid.go.th/kmc08/km_59/ manual_59/Book6/The-Fift--Discipline.pdf

CHAPTER 15

New Teaching-Learning Methodologies Globalization

Srinivasa Babu Ampalam[1,*] and **Pulakhandam Srinivasa Rao**[1]

[1] *Gayatri College of Science and Management Srikakulam, Dr. B.R. Ambedkar University, Srikakulam, Andhra Pradesh, India*

Abstract: Quality is highly required in the present teaching and learning process besides quantity. Nobody is expected to get contentment without quality in our life or career. Innovation is given utmost importance in higher education in the present global world. National Assessment and Accreditation Council (NAAC) was established to fulfill all these aspects in higher educational institutions. It has stipulated certain procedures for assessing and preparing students as well as teachers to make them competent enough to face the challenges in the present day global scenario. The teachers need to update their knowledge and use new methods effectively in the classroom sessions to give a new shape to the students. We have to carry this responsibility until we get retirement. For many decades, we followed the traditional method of using textbooks for the purpose of instruction. However, the emergence and implementation of teaching effectiveness assessment techniques revealed that most of the students do not equip themselves with course content up to the expected level. The Majority of intellectuals focus on new methods for teaching and learning processes. Our teaching or learning methods should be intelligible. The objective of this chapter is to mention the importance of innovative teaching and learning methods and study the understanding of changes by teachers and also the need for refresher courses for teachers at regular intervals. A teacher may be a facilitator in the present teaching and learning scenario. The new methods must certainly be useful to both the students and the teachers to do research and also develop creativity. The teaching fraternity may agree with the new methods in the teaching and learning process.

Keywords: Academic audit, Attitude, Contentment, Creativity, Facilitator, Future challenges, Globalization, Imparting knowledge, Innovation NAAC, NAAC, New methodologies, Profession by choice, Quality, Teaching and learning process, Technology, Traditional, Vital role.

---

[*] **Corresponding author Srinivasa Babu Ampalam:** Gayatri College of Science and Management Srikakulam, Dr. B.R. Ambedkar University, Srika-kulam, Andhra Pradesh, India; Tel: 9989818084;
E-mail: srinivaskalpanaa@gmail.com

Sankara Narayana Rao Gedala and P.L. Saranya (Eds)
All rights reserved-© 2021 Bentham Science Publishers

INTRODUCTION

Education doesn't mean dumping some information into the student's brain without assessing their capacity to grasp it. In this case, a teacher must be a good psychologist to know the methods suitable according to the needs of the students in the present globalization. The student utilizes this knowledge to lead his/her life in a splendid way. The teaching must be student-centric and should involve the students during the process of learning. The teachers have to show scope to students for innovation in teaching instead of traditional ways of teaching. Enthusiasm should be created among the students. The students should be involved in all kinds of activities, and the teaching should be activity-based. The students are prepared to pay attention to research-oriented activities besides textual knowledge. They are supposed to take everything challenging during their lifetime. Life skills are to be taught by all the teachers besides their subject. It is the prime responsibility of the teachers to see the students make use of digital classrooms and send them to different places to enhance their life skills.

Every teacher is to be competent enough to teach necessary skills besides their subjects by using methodologies that are suitable to that particular context. In this context, teachers are to be given training in different areas. The new methodologies are to be adopted to impart the knowledge through our teaching and students make use of applications of the theory they have learned so far. This chapter mainly focuses on unique teaching methods for the betterment and prosperity of the students in the present state of globalization.

Teaching and learning methods at the undergraduate level can be very different. How you teach will largely depend on your course content and level of study. The learning process should be student-centric. The new methods should be useful to the students in terms of creating interest in a particular topic or area of study. Then only, students are expected to get contentment. In this connection, we motivate the students to come out of rote learning. This rote learning basically depends on memory. The student may understand or may not understand the explanation given by the teacher concerned. This type of learning cannot be useful to lead his or her life comfortably and secure a better position in society.

In the present state of globalization, students are encouraged to participate in fruitful discussions on any area they have read in the class or independently, weighing its merits or considering its application. They are expected to get equipped with practical knowledge besides theoretical knowledge. It's better to avoid providing study materials to the students. Instead of this, the teacher should enable the students to prepare notes on their own to pay attention to the lecture given by the teacher in the classroom on a particular topic. Discussions are an important part of the teaching-learning process. This gives the students, not only access to other viewpoints on the same subject matter but also enabling them to consider different rationale and logic, hugely important elements of professional post-study life. Most of the students hail from rural areas is the basic thing or barrier in the state-funded colleges. They may not be good at communication skills. The teacher has to motivate them to participate in interactions either in their mother tongue or English. I ensure that they gradually enrich their skills. We have to provide a platform for them. Learning by doing is an essential part of the study. The students are asked to work independently, in pairs, or as part of a small team for most of the courses. We have to consider that practice during the course work.

It is also an essential way of learning. It should be implemented in a unique way. Problem based or inquiry-based learning is an important strategy to bring practice into the classroom. We have to give a problem to the student which pertains to real-life or ask students to make an inquiry to get the results connecting with your life. This way of learning enables students to get equipped with life skills. Nowadays, many of the students are lagging in this area. It has a high potential. If necessary, some project works should be given to the students.

Technology is advancing in our day to day life in the present times. In this connection, E-learning plays a vital role in the present education system. The teachers, as well as the students, are in a dire need to take training in this perspective. Many institutions now have a virtual learning environment of some sort. The students are required to study online, using material created by the teachers, download papers and take online tests, or access relevant audio and video material. In this technical age, many institutions around the world are creating technology-rich learning spaces across campuses, including access to a wide range of digital resources available even at the undergraduate level of study.

The students are motivated and involved in co-curricular activities. Interest should be created among all the students and make them participate in those activities. Certainly, they would not be affected by stress management. Involvement of students in co-curricular activities is another way for students to build upon the knowledge, skills, and abilities they develop in their graduate-level programs. Further, they develop their soft skills. Student, career and professional clubs, internships, voluntary activities, work projects, diverse, multicultural events, and academic competitions are the most common co-curricular activities in which students are involved. The teacher always welcomes new ideas from the students. An open-minded attitude can help the teacher in innovating new teaching methods.

The teachers are not confined to old traditional methods only. They also try to find out new methods that are useful in imparting knowledge to the students besides using the methods formally recommended by the apex bodies like Commissionerate of Collegiate Education. The teacher's main objective is to make the students lead their life in a splendid way. Stimulating environment is to be created in the classroom. It will help stimulate a student's mind to think and learn better. Such a creative and stimulating environment will help them explore new knowledge and will encourage them to learn about the subject. We have to organize social, networking and cultural activities. Project based learning in the classroom is also to be initiated. Such methods cater to the needs of the students.

Knowledge is to be extracted through reading from the teacher's mono-log through visual perception or discussion in the classroom. Smart Classroom teaching or technology certainly brings a change in our mode of learning through living. It also influences other people in many aspects. We can find some behavioral changes among the people. Teachers inculcate the habit of adopting the use of all available sources of learning like tech-environment, android phones, video games, video lessons, relevant TV programs *etc.* The outcome of this is that the students are expected to reach the great pinnacles of their life. Competence and present-oriented approaches have been introduced. Student-centered learning, the introduction of curriculum standards, decentralization of educational finance and governance, the priority of higher education, standardization of student assessment, and liberalization of textbook publishing is to be incorporated judiciously. The textbook is to be framed by a team of experts by keeping the level of students understanding in mind and it should create an impression that it will certainly be useful in the future.

The teachers should be dynamic and enthusiastic about improving pedagogical skills and mastering innovations and novelty in teaching. The teaching-learning process has components of purpose and learning objectives, content, methods, teaching tools, learning forms, and results. These should be carefully included while we are planning lesson plans for teaching plans. We should also identify the drastic changes related to multimedia and the introduction of it in the educational environment. Lang's solution is 'small teaching'. Rather than a whole change, he proposes techniques that you can read about in the evening and implement the next morning in your lecture class. An example is given using predictions in class. Students are given some evidence of what they will encounter in the next week's class and asked to make their best guess about its meaning. When they expected it and asked to reflect on it at greater length the following week, the researcher material was more confidential. I do it for my students and get fruitful results. A practical approach is more useful than a theoretical approach. The students are actively involved in each and every learning activity. Then only will they become active instead of passive. The teacher better asks the students to write summaries of the main points of each lecture at its conclusion, writing five-minute reflections after discussions.

Many rapid changes in these days have caused the Higher Education system to face a great variety of challenges. In this context, training is an essential component. Thoughtful individuals in interdisciplinary fields are required. The students are prepared to learn something with research-oriented bent up of mind. A lot of priority is to be given to research work. There has always been an emphasis on equal attention to research and teaching quality and establishing a bond between these two. Any new methodology is to be introduced by keeping this point in view only. Teaching and learning in higher education is a shared process, with responsibilities on both student and teacher to contribute to their success. Within this shared process, higher education must engage the students in questioning their preconceived ideas and their models of how the world works, so that they can reach a higher level of understanding. But students are always thinking about the highest scoring in terms of marks in the public examinations. The teacher's prime responsibility is to make students realize the fact and be able to face future challenges. New teaching methods such as student-centered active methods, problem based and project-based approaches are highly useful to the teachers to impart the knowledge to the students. The problem –oriented approach, in addition to improved communication skills among students, not only increased development critical thinking but also promoted study skills and an interest in their learning. The students are given the liberty to learn at their own choice. We should not stop them and confine them to our ideas only in the teaching-learning process, logging progress on class projects, going back to earlier entries and annotating or updating with new ideas, and so on.

The present generation has lost reading habits. We inculcate the habit of reading journals among the students to get the acquisition of more knowledge. The idea of keeping a journal for a class put in a different mindset for the class. It opened up a space for me in my own thinking to reflect on what we were learning and discussing as we were learning it, which really enhanced my class experience. Inevitably some students will do the bare minimum, but many others will create beautiful, richly annotated records of their learning. This type of learning certainly bears a fruitful result to the students (Dannelle D. Stevens, 2009).

Assigning study projects to the students as a group. The liberty is to be given to the students to make a choice of a topic. The teacher has to allow the students to select the topic of the project, which is to be connected to the lives of the students besides their interest. They are also relevant to what the students planned to do after college. The students are encouraged and motivated to do a case study on the basis of their interested area. With this, they will be closer to society and equip themselves with life skills. Some readers may want to skip the chapters, jumping straight from the introduction to the conclusion. The book's last chapter functions as a powerful blueprint for shaping writing assignments that build students' motivation and make for a memorable and meaningful learning experience. This method certainly enlightens the students.

There are many ways to involve and engage students in many activities, both inside and outside the classroom. Miller 's argument is essentially threefold: students use classroom technology for the betterment of knowledge and they have less work. Her book is an inspiring one to the teachers. Her book gives excellent suggestions for making better use of learning management systems like canvas, moodle and blackboard, experimenting with real-time polling; and encouraging digital-born projects for course assignments. I have learnt that testing helps the students to recall information. I made simple quizzes manually and later changed them into online ones. I applied for the subject of English. It's not possible for me to conduct at regular intervals due to some technical constraints. But we have succeeded to some extent in this regard. Students really enjoyed themselves very much. They scored well with a lot of contentment. This method of learning is also good for the betterment of the students.

New developments show the relationship between society and universities has been altering in recent years. What methods we use at present are not permanent and they are tentative. We should adopt the methods according to the needs of the students and the expectations of the world. That's why the old saying "a teacher is always a student". He has to update the knowledge and adopt the methods which are suitable to the students at that time. Students must be linked with society and they have to contribute something for the prosperity of society. Expansion of knowledge is certainly as powerful as impetus to innovation as the exposition of numbers, and its scale has been graphically expressed in many ways. The growth and diversification of knowledge are also expressed in curricular terms – in the changing content of the courses that students are expected to follow (Michele Eodice, 2017). As the repository of knowledge expands and alters, the curriculum must be adapted and new maps of learning must be drawn. The fact that many of the growing points of knowledge in recent years are found at the intersection of traditional disciplines is one of the factors presenting interdisciplinary inquiry; at the same time the need to reflect these new intellectual relationships in the course structure is expressed in a movement towards interdisciplinary teaching. But this is not all.

From the standpoint of the learner, what matters most is not the formal instruction he is given but the kind of learning resources to which he has access, and also the range of competencies he acquires which will enable him to make good use of the resources to fulfill his aims. We should equip ourselves with newly available resources during the process of learning and teaching (James M.Lang, 2016). Apart from the motives for creating a new curriculum pattern, one must note the impact of students' demands for relevance in their courses, which is as much part of the dynamics of higher education today as such external pressures as the skilled manpower needs of a society and its changing employment patterns.

Many obstacles may appear on the path of such attempts to reform the curriculum, organizational, teaching methods and evaluation. Quite different organizing concepts and operating skills may be required for both faculty and students for the new curriculum patterns. Besides all these things, ideal teachers should inculcate the awareness in developing certain best qualities like cooperation, coordination, leadership, adjustment behavior, compassion towards the poorest of the poor, teamwork, good communication skills to meet the future challenges, organizing skills, social responsibility, motivation, human values and their significance, human relationships, gender justice, life skills and the most significant aspect personality development *etc*. We pave the way to the students reaching their destiny. The additional curriculum is to be designed with innovative practices to cater to the present needs of the students.

Quality analysis is made for the effectiveness of a teacher through the new methods used by the individual teacher. We also conduct surveys by using a student feedback system. Through which we can give the knowledge which keeps the student by reaching great pinnacles of life. The higher education ranking of the Universities is based on the quality of teaching-learning environment. This chapter helps to understand the requirement of the learning environment in the institutes.

CONCLUSION

The above mentioned new methods may be useful for effective teaching and learning in the present state of globalization. Everything is to be planned and executed for the interest of the learner. The teachers are required to attend the training programs and update their skills in teaching. They may use some innovative methods in their way. The final objective is to justify their duty to the students to give the knowledge that is useful to lead their life in a splendid way.

CONSENT FOR PUBLICATION

Not applicable.

CONFLICT OF INTEREST

The author declares no conflict of interest, financial or otherwise.

ACKNOWLEDGEMENTS

Declared none.

REFERENCES

Aigirian, M. (2017). Zukhra sadavaloawora: pedagogy of the twenty first century innovative teaching methods – Aigirian Mynbayova. *Zukhra Sadavaloawora*.
[http://dx.doi.org/10.5772/INTECHOPEN.72341]

Dannelle, D.S., Joanne, E. (2009). Cooper journal keeping: how to use reflective writing for learning, teaching, professional insight, and positive change. (p. 266). Sterling, VA: Stylus.
[http://dx.doi.org/10.1111/j.1467-9647.2010.00656.x]

James, M. (2016). Lang: small teaching everyday lessons from the science of learning. Wiley. https://isbnsearch.org/isbn/9781118944493

Michele, E. (2017). Meaningful writing project learning, teaching and writing in higher education. University press of Colarado, Utah State University Press. https://www.jstor.org/stable/j.ctt1kc6hjg

Miller, D. (2016). Minds online: teaching effectively with technology. Harvard University Press. https://isbnsearch.org/isbn/9780674660021

SUBJECT INDEX

A

Academia-industry interactions 28
Academic 1, 4, 21, 32, 52, 80, 83, 145, 147
   activities 1, 4, 21, 32, 52, 80
   audit 145
   competitions 147
   reputation survey 83
Academicians 26, 33
   eminent 26
Accountability and performance of teachers 131
Accreditation 8, 25, 26, 34, 53, 84, 91, 145
   automated 91
   council 8, 25, 34, 145
   process 26, 53, 84
Accrediting bodies 82, 83, 85
Activities 4, 11, 14, 16, 30, 40, 62, 86, 141, 146, 148
   cultural 148
   extracurricular 4, 11, 14, 16, 30, 40
   institutional 86
   professional 141
   research-oriented 146
   violent 62
Advanced controlled design systems 68
All India council for technical education (AICTE) 119, 134, 135
Alumni 6, 90
   engagement 90
   support 6
Analysis 28, 31, 98
   comparative 98
   drinking water 31
   rank score 101
   systematic 28
Analytical reasoning 131
Ancient history records 116
Annual 31, 61, 62
   quality assurance reports (AQAR) 31
   Status of education report (ASER) 61, 62
Autonomic nervous system 72

Awareness campaigns 6

B

Bachelors degree 68

C

Candidates 70, 71, 123
   job interviews 70
   prospective 71
   qualified 123
Career guidance 126
Child marriages 29
Children 29, 52, 62, 63, 64
   disabled 29
Choice-based credit system (CBCS) 25, 28
Class 55, 149
   assignments 55
   projects 149
Classroom 9, 13, 16, 17, 30, 33, 48, 100, 140, 141, 142, 145, 146, 147, 148, 150
   overcrowded 100
   sessions 145
   structure 33
   teaching 30, 33
   virtual 9
   technology 150
   time 48
Collaboration 2, 29, 30, 32, 107, 108, 109, 110, 112, 126, 134, 137, 138
   research-industry 2
Collaborative research initiatives 89
College(s) 4, 6, 26, 34, 39, 40, 41, 99, 118, 125, 130, 147
   affiliated 34, 125, 130
   assessed 26
   engineering 99
   feedback process 6
   medical 99
   in rural areas 4
   libraries 6

management 41
private 34, 36, 39, 40
rural 6
sector 26
semi-urban 6
state-funded 147
Collegiate competitions 30
Communication technology 80
Community 3, 6, 29, 32, 47, 87
local 6
Companies, multinational 132
Competition 3, 62, 100, 113
foreign 113
global 100
Competitive 90, 132
examinations 90
levels, global 132
Computer programming 68
Congenial work ambience 78
Cooperative learning techniques 142
Coordinators, institutions IQAC 31
Cost reduction 91, 94
Council 2, 42, 43, 135
for scientific and industrial research (CSIR) 2, 42, 43
of architecture (COA) 135
Courses 3, 6, 27, 77, 92
certificate/diploma 27
degree 77
interdisciplinary 3, 6
online 92
professional 129, 132
Cumulative grade point average (CGPA) 31, 35, 37
Customer buying decision 54

D

Data 56, 80, 84, 89, 95
gathering 89
handling 84
institutional 80
management 95
retrieval 56

validation and verification (DVV) 80, 84
Degrees 5, 109, 94, 110, 112
doctorate 5
foreign 109, 110, 112
globally-recognized 94
Developing 49, 81
employability skills 49
skilled manpower 81
Development organizations 99
Digital
classrooms 57, 146
data bases 4
organization culture 54
scholarship 54
technologies 55, 81
Diploma level 119
nursing institutes 119
teacher training institutes 119
technical institutes 119
District institute of education and training (DIETs) 119

E

Early childhood care 64
Economic 53, 56, 61, 115, 122
forum 61
issues 53, 56
survey 115, 122
Education 55, 61, 63, 64, 128, 131, 134
free 134
modern 55
play-based 61, 63, 64
skill-oriented 128
value-based qualitative 131
Educational 66, 100, 125
hub 100, 125
learning stages 66
Educational institutions 35, 65, 116, 118, 120, 121, 122, 123, 129, 138
modern 116
modern higher 116
private 123, 129
Education 2, 62, 110

ministry 2
policies 110
survey 62
Education system 34, 39, 52, 58, 61, 62, 87, 109, 110, 112, 126, 130
progressive 52
Effective problem solving skills 72
EFQM excellence model 81
Electronic literacy 54
Emotional intelligence 58, 67, 72, 73, 75
Employability skills 9, 14, 16, 17, 19, 68, 69
Employer reputation survey 83
Employment opportunities 1, 119
English speaking people 2
Environment 61, 64, 67, 78, 104, 126, 142, 148
changing 67
educational 148
emerging economic 78
Environmental 31, 62
consciousness 31
degradation 62
Evaluation 26, 27, 28, 36, 51, 53, 58, 82, 83, 87, 89, 131, 151
data-based quantitative indicator 26
systems 131
Examination 10, 33, 48, 87, 89, 95
common entrance 48
department 95
pattern 33
Exchange 100, 113
international academic 113

F

Facilities 17, 30, 122, 131
communication lab 17
hygienic food 48
infrastructural 122
library 30, 122
physical 131
Feedback 6, 9, 10, 11, 15, 18, 19, 21, 25, 26, 27, 28, 71
constructive 71

multiple 19
process 6, 10, 19, 21
Fee 4, 130
reimbursement benefits 130
structure 4
Financial 2, 42, 108, 109, 112
assistance 2
deficit 42
investment 108, 109, 112
Food, natural 143
Formats 9, 15, 21, 81, 90, 95
heterogeneous 81
student feedback analysis 15
Framework, enabled model 95
Freelance writer 57

G

Garg's operational excellence model 81
GIS-based system 54
Globalization 100, 113
of higher education 100
process 113
Global standards 1, 2, 3
Government 1, 3, 4, 77, 121, 126, 135, 139
of India (GOI) 1, 3, 4, 77, 121, 126, 135
policy 139
Gross domestic product 42
Gross 1, 3, 43, 46, 86, 120, 121, 122, 128, 136
enrollment ratio (GER) 1, 3, 46, 86, 120, 121, 122, 128, 136
national income (GNI) 43
Growth, economic 42, 78, 115, 131, 138

H

Higher education 1, 2, 3, 99, 100, 115, 118, 119, 121, 122, 123, 125, 127, 128, 135
global 100
level 119
policy 99, 122
system 1, 2, 3, 99, 100, 115, 118, 121, 123, 125, 127, 128, 135
Hotel management 119

Human 1, 42, 43, 44, 49, 80, 87, 115, 128, 129, 151
   development index (HDI) 42, 43, 44
   relationships 151
   resources 1, 49, 80, 87, 115, 128, 129

I

ICT-enabled 89
   facilities 89
   enabled grievance readdress systems 89
Independent regulatory authority for higher education (IRAHE) 4
India 62, 118, 129, 135
   educating rural 62
   globalized economy 129
   survey on higher education 118
Indian council 2, 135
   of historical research (ICHR) 135
   of medical research (ICMR) 2, 135
   of philosophical research (ICPR) 135
Indian nursing council 119
India's 116, 120
   education system 116
   gross enrollment ratio 120
Information and communication technology (ICT) 8, 9, 10, 25, 26, 80, 81, 86, 87, 88, 89, 90, 92, 93, 95
Infrastructure, digital 53
Infrastructure facilities 2, 122, 125, 127
   academic 2
   educational 125
Institutes 1, 2, 3, 4, 5, 6, 8, 9, 10, 11, 21, 34, 35, 40, 119, 126, 132
   academic 11, 21
   accrediting 40
   international 126, 132
   present domestic 113
   private 3
   second-grade 1
   third-grade government 132
   world-class 2, 3
Interdisciplinary programs 1

Internal quality assurance cell (IQAC) 8, 9, 25, 27, 31, 36
International science policy 83

L

Learning 9, 26, 29, 30, 48, 49, 56, 66, 69, 86, 87, 89, 99, 116, 118, 142, 145, 146, 150
   digital 56
   experimental 69
   higher 26, 99, 116, 118
   interpersonal skills 142
   lifelong 86
   management system (LMS) 9, 30, 89, 150
   methods, problem-solving-based 48
   process 29, 145, 146
   project-based 48, 49
   research-based 66
   resource system 87
Learning skills 48, 68, 77
   developing long-term 48
Life 63, 65, 67, 72, 73, 74, 75, 136, 137, 138, 145, 146, 147, 148, 151
   professional post-study 147
   student's 138
Life expectancy index 43
Lifelong learning experience enriches 65
Logging progress 149

M

Machine learning 52
Management 4, 30, 31, 32, 36, 42, 53, 62, 81, 90, 91, 93, 94, 99, 119, 121, 131
   committees 62
   financial 31
   human resource 42
   information system (MIS) 81, 91, 93, 94
   studies 99, 121
   wastewater 31
Mapping of intended educational objectives 89
Methods 10, 131, 145, 148, 149
   electronic format questionnaire 10

student-centered active 149
traditional 131, 145, 148
Ministry of human resource development (MHRD) 53, 121, 126
Modern technology 61
Modern tools 87
Multinational corporations 100
Multi-perspective hypermedia environment 54

N

NAAC methodology 27, 36
and Challenges of HEI 27
National 1, 6, 36, 83, 88, 95, 100, 108, 109, 112, 119, 132, 135
council for teacher education (NCTE) 119
council of rural institute (NCRI) 135
education policy 100, 108, 109, 112
institute ranking framework (NIRF) 1, 6, 36, 83, 88, 95
knowledge commission 132
NIRF's 6
credibility 6
website 6

O

ODL 86
education 86
programs 86
Online 9, 10
learning management systems 9
student feedback system 10
Optional metrics-rules & regulations 31
Organizations 56, 67, 76, 80, 90, 136, 137
competitive 90
large business 76

P

Perception 40, 62, 81, 82, 101, 148
parental 40
reputation survey/peer 82
visual 148

Period, industrial revolution 49
Philanthropists 6
Planning lesson plans 148
Policies 21, 34, 81, 112, 126, 134, 135
national 34, 112
Policy 5, 9, 90, 100
decisions 9
formulation 90
makers 5, 100
Policy measures 98, 100, 101, 109, 110, 111, 112
GITAM University 110
Population 5, 29, 43, 94, 101, 115, 116, 122, 125, 132, 137
global 94
growing 132
huge 125
productive 116
working age 125
Private 38, 39, 48
degree colleges 38, 39
sector companies 48
Procedures, digital 3
Process 8, 10, 25, 26, 55, 56, 65, 66, 69, 81, 82, 83, 84, 85, 97, 94, 141
interactive 141
non-academic 83, 87
Productivity 83, 116
academic 83
Professional 89, 147
clubs 147
development programmes 89
Programs 3, 18, 28, 29, 32, 48, 61, 62, 99, 118, 119, 120, 134, 135, 137, 138, 147
certificate 119
colleges run Post Graduate 118
for international student assessment (PISA) 61, 62
graduate-level 147
health awareness 29
running single 118
undergraduate 48
Project 28, 68
management 68
works, research-based 28

Public universities 101, 112
Pupil teacher ratio (PTR) 120

Q

QS 53, 83
  ranking system 83
  world ranking focus 53
Quality 49, 81, 82, 115, 123
  assurance processes 82
  education 49, 81, 115, 123
Quantitative metrics 27
  criteria 27
  online 27

R

Ranking 6, 66, 84, 85, 86, 90, 91, 94
  framework organization 6
  processes 66, 84, 85, 86, 90, 91, 94
Research 2, 3, 4, 81, 82, 83, 89, 90, 94, 99, 107, 108, 112, 116, 118, 121, 125, 126, 128, 131, 137
  collaborative 126
  innovations 107, 108, 112
  outcomes 81, 82, 89, 90
Resources 3, 4, 29, 42, 44, 80, 87, 91, 94, 98, 113, 115, 130, 147, 151
  digital 3, 147
  inadequate material 100
  natural 42, 44, 115
  raising revenue 113
Respective gross domestic products 42
Revolution 53
  digital 53
  industrial 53

S

Scenario 2, 145
  global 145
  global academic 2

Score of reform factors of higher education 104, 105, 108, 109
Sectors 43, 44, 45, 47, 53, 98, 107, 108, 112, 125, 128, 134, 137, 138, 139
  agricultural 43
  corporate 107, 108, 112
  educational 125
Self 27, 32, 73
  assessment 73
  awareness 73
  study reports (SSR) 27, 32
Semester system 4
Services 2, 5, 29, 47, 53, 81, 98, 100, 101, 102, 110, 111, 112
  better education 112
  cloud 5
Skill(s) 9, 42, 53, 64, 69, 70, 102, 103, 105, 12
  aural 70
  decision-making 64
  development courses in colleges 69
  development programs 9, 102
  persuasive 69
  personality development programs 105
  teaching 53, 142
Smart classroom teaching 148
Smartphones 6, 51, 53
Social media 52, 53, 56, 57, 69
  Manager 57
  marketing platforms 56
  platforms 53
Society 3, 5, 53, 54, 63, 66, 118, 121, 125, 128, 129, 135, 136, 142, 150, 151
  contemporary 3, 5
  democratic 142
Socio-cultural background 10
Socioeconomic background 62
Staff 26, 27, 30, 31, 32, 69, 95, 125
  non-teaching 95, 125
  proactive 27
State council for education research and training (SCERT) 119
Statistical techniques 91
Stress 76, 77
  inadequate 134
Stress management 76, 147

Structure-function relations 99
Student 3, 4, 10, 11, 35, 36, 54, 55, 58, 148
   centered concepts 35
   centered education and dynamic methods 4
   centered Learning 54, 55, 148
   satisfaction survey 11
   evaluation of teaching effectiveness rating scale 10
   job opportunities 3
   support system 35, 36
   teacher relationships 58
Success 11, 39, 62, 65, 67, 73, 75, 76, 77, 81, 139, 149
   mercantile 39
   professional 67
Survey 5, 10
   questionnaire 10
   reports 5
System 26, 28, 30, 33, 37, 52, 54, 57, 81, 83, 89, 90, 93, 126, 142, 150
   automatic checks/alarming 90
   choice based credit 89
   enabled Bio-metric 126
   generated scores (SGS) 26
   learning management 30, 89, 150

T

Teachers 51, 142
   agency 51
   effective 142
Teaching 10, 48, 107, 108, 112, 145, 150
   and learning process 145
   effectiveness rating scale 10
   innovative 48, 145
   interdisciplinary 150
   modern academic 107, 108, 112
Teaching-learning 21, 52, 63, 81, 129
   activities 21
   facilities 81
   financing 129
   online resource materials 52
   process implementing concepts 63

Teaching 13, 16, 17, 87, 129, 140, 141, 148, 149
   plans 148
   process 13, 16, 17
   quality 129, 149
   staff 87
   strategies 140, 141
   techniques 140, 141
Techniques 76, 145
   relaxation 76
   teaching effectiveness assessment 145
Technology-rich learning spaces 147
Telecommunications 81
Training 100, 102, 151
   facilities 100
   programs 102, 151
Transferring information 78
t-tests 92, 101

U

University grants commission (UGC) 1, 2, 42, 43, 69, 121, 122, 126, 130, 134, 135

V

Video 147, 148
   lessons 148
   material 147
Virtual 51, 132
   classroom-teaching 132
   connectivity 51

W

Web 56, 57, 68
   based information resources 56
   Developer 57
   development 68
Webinars sessions 57
Web of Science 84

www.ingramcontent.com/pod-product-compliance
Lightning Source LLC
Chambersburg PA
CBHW041152290426
44108CB00002B/41